The
Tai Chi
Bible

八卦周天圖

見 愚 天 體 此 萬
三 蒙 機 種 是 叁
。

The

Tai Chi
Bible

The definitive guide to
decoding the Tai Chi form

Dan Docherty

FIREFLY BOOKS

A FIREFLY BOOK

Published by Firefly Books Ltd. 2014

First printing

**Publisher Cataloging-in-Publication Data
(U.S.)**

A CIP record for this title is available from
the Library of Congress

**Library and Archives Canada Cataloguing
in Publication**

A CIP record for this title is available from
Library and Archives Canada

Published in the United States by
Firefly Books (U.S.) Inc.
P.O. Box 1338, Ellicott Station
Buffalo, New York 14205

Published in Canada by
Firefly Books Ltd.
50 Staples Avenue, Unit 1
Richmond Hill, Ontario L4B 0A7

Printed in China

Any information given in this book
is not intended to be taken as a
replacement for medical advice. Any
person with a condition requiring
medical attention should consult a
qualified practitioner or therapist.

Conceived, designed, and produced by
Godsfield Press, a division of Octopus Publishing
Group Ltd
Endeavour House, 189 Shaftesbury Avenue
London WC2H 8JY
www.octopusbooks.co.uk

Publisher   Liz Dean
Deputy Art Director   Yasia Williams-Leedham
Design   Geoff Borin
Photography   Russell Sadur
Editors   Alex Stetter and Katy Denny
Models   Catherine Birkinhead, Rae Brunton,
Clifford Cox, Kathy Davies, Stephen Davies, Neil
Farnan, Damien Hoadley-Brown, Gabriella Kosa,
Ladan Niayesh, Mark Paterson, Jason Tsang

Contents

Foreword

Tai Chi is a paradox. Its image with the media and the general public is that it is some kind of moving meditation, a bit like yoga. It's done slowly. It's easy to learn. It's effortless. It's about breathing. All of these images are partially accurate.

Tai Chi can involve holding static postures. There can be sharp and sudden movement. Tai Chi can involve the Chinese internal alchemy practices that influenced Kundalini yoga. Learning to do Tai Chi really well is neither easy nor effortless for most people. It's about correct posture and smooth movement, which are the prerequisites for correct breathing.

Tai Chi is a highly effective system of self defence as it relies on skill and evasion, as demonstrated on pages 36–227. Concepts, drills and techniques used in Tai Chi self defence can be easily adopted by practitioners of other arts such as karate and judo and help improve their understanding and effectiveness. Sports people from soccer, golf, tennis and other sports have told me how Tai Chi practice has raised their mental and physical game and improved their technique.

Tai Chi practise relaxes the body and improves the balance and coordination. This helps to prevent falls – the most common reason for the elderly to attend the Accident and Emergency Department in hospitals. Tai Chi practise also leads to better respiration and circulation. I have taught many asthmatics who were able to give up their inhalers after some weeks of daily practice. Regular Tai Chi practise helps with Type 2 Diabetes; my Tai Chi master had type 1, and it helped him too. Those who suffer from heart problems, arthritis and conditions such as Parkinson's (I was diagnosed in 2011) can also benefit greatly from the daily practice of Tai Chi.

Tai Chi is for all and it has a lot to offer as this book shows. The equation is simple. Firstly find a suitable teacher and method; secondly, practise every day. I wish you every success with Tai Chi.

Author Dan Docherty (left) demonstrates a drill to two students of Tai Chi.

Introduction

The mission

The primary mission of this book is to inform readers exactly what Tai Chi involves and to give them enough detail so that they can try it for themselves. The secondary mission is to engage the experienced student and teacher by furnishing them with information that is not readily available elsewhere, such as the Tai Chi syllabus (see pages 376–386), 'Errant Knights' (see pages 276–339) and 'Inner Form' material (see pages 96 and 104).

This volume traces the origin and development of the Chinese art of Tai Chi Chuan (which translates as 'Supreme Ultimate Fist') in the interactions of the two equal and opposite principles known as Yin and Yang, as described in the *Book of Changes* more than three thousand years ago and examines how this duality was used from early times in Chinese martial arts and breathing exercises.

It discusses each of the major aspects of the Tai Chi syllabus, including weapons (see pages 284–339), internal strength (see pages 46–75), pushing hands (see pages 46–75) as well as hand forms and application and their interrelationship; this book also covers key concepts from the five Tai Chi Chuan Classics, which govern the practice of all styles of Tai Chi. The solo hand-form sequences of choreographed movements are what most people who have ever seen or practised Tai Chi are most familiar with. Thousands of variations of hand forms are being practised, but they almost all trace their origins to the Yang or Chen lineages, with Yang-lineage styles being more common.

I teach a popular variation of Yang-lineage Tai Chi, known as Wu style. I call my approach 'Practical Tai Chi Chuan'. With the help of illustrations I will explain in detail each of the most common Tai Chi techniques (and some more obscure ones) and their function, with reference (where it can be found) to the Ming-dynasty book, *The Classic of Boxing*, and to Chinese myth and legend. Beginners will benefit from practising the postures, while advanced practitioners of all styles will gain greater insight into their regular practice. Similarly, using the principle that every movement has its function, the book decodes an 'Inner Form' of lost or hidden techniques.

From my experience of teaching Chinese concepts to thousands of students throughout the world over a great many years, I try to give down-to-earth advice on Tai Chi practice, which will be of use to novice and adept alike. I have romanized most of the Chinese names and terminology according to the official pinyin system used in mainland China, but where an alternative is more common I have used that — for example, Tai Chi for Taiji and Kung Fu for Gongfu.

Finally, any art is about personalities; and so, hoping to entertain as well as to inform, I have included some tales of Tai Chi masters from the past (see pages 358–367), including my own Sifu, Cheng Tin-hung.

Diagram of Three Potentialities; Heaven above and Earth below with Humanity in the centre, harmonizing with both.

From Tai Chi to Tai Chi Chuan

So what does the term 'Tai Chi Chuan' actually mean?

The character *Tai* means 'supreme' or 'extreme', so the Chinese term for wife, *Tai Tai*, means 'supremely supreme'. The character *Chi* means 'ultimate' or 'pole' (as in North/South Pole). The combination of the two characters *Tai Chi* first appeared in Chinese literature in about 200 BCE in an appendix to the *Yi Jing/I Ching* (the *Book of Changes*) and is considered to be the supreme principle of the universe and the source of change. And the character Chuan means 'fist' and, by extension, 'boxing' or 'martial art'.

Tai Chi Chuan should therefore be the martial art of change, although this is not the perception that most Western practitioners have.

Chinese philosophy and Tai Chi

The three most important schools of Chinese philosophy are Confucianism (named after Confucius), Buddhism (named after the Buddha) and Taoism (named after the Chinese term for 'the Way/Ways'). They are often referred to collectively as 'The Three Teachings'.

Confucius was mainly concerned with the morality and propriety that were expected of a gentleman, though he encouraged other manly pursuits, such as archery and charioteering. Confucianism influenced Chinese martial arts in giving them a code of conduct and a family-style hierarchy. The teacher is therefore called Shifu/Sifu (meaning 'teaching father'), while the Tudi ('disciples') address one another as 'Elder/Younger Brother/Sister'. In many schools there is a Confucian-influenced ritual initiation ceremony for disciples.

The Chinese imported Buddhism from India. It was based on compassion and on attempting to achieve enlightenment. Chan (Japanese Zen) Buddhism was of particular significance for Chinese martial arts because the patriarch Bodhidharma founded the famous Shaolin Temple in 527 CE, which promoted meditation and hygienic exercise, as well as so-called 'external martial arts'. Chan Buddhism and the Complete Reality School of Taoism greatly influenced one another, especially in the fields of meditation and philosophy.

Philosophical Taoism was concerned with living in harmony with the environment and attaining the Way through alchemy, exercise, meditation and martial arts, in places like Wudang Mountain, where once (around the 14th century CE) the Tai Chi patriarch Zhang Sanfeng dwelt. No matter what the exact truth is concerning the origins of Tai Chi, the theory comes largely from philosophical Taoism. There was even a Tai Chi Diagram sect in the 11th century CE.

Cluster of temples and priest residences on Golden Summit of Wudang Mountain.

Chinese holistic exercise and Tai Chi

Chinese health exercises, both moving and static, are largely based on animals and birds. They date back to at least the 5th century BCE, as there are references to them in the works of the Taoist philosophers Laozi and Zhuangzi and manuals were available at around the same time. We refer to them now as Qigong/Chi Kung (vital energy/breath training) and Neigong/Nei Kung (internal training). Many Tai Chi techniques are also based on animals, and much of the theory on posture and movement is similar to that found in those early manuals.

Such exercises were sometimes meditative, sometimes martial; sometimes therapeutic, ritualistic or performed as an internal alchemy. Ideally Tai Chi practice combines all of these approaches.

Chinese meditation and Tai Chi

The Chinese have a myriad of different approaches to meditation, many of which are explained in detailed manuals. It is rarely clear, even to the expert, where the lines are to be drawn between internal alchemy, holistic exercise and meditation; it is mainly a question of where the emphasis lies.

Tai Chi is sometimes described as 'moving meditation', although it can be static as well as moving – in particular form techniques and in Neigong (see pages 31–34). It is remarkable for its versatility. In meditation Tai Chi has a multiplicity of purposes, combining elements of ritual, martial arts, holistic exercise, internal alchemy, philosophy in action and spirituality.

Two views of the Forbidden City

Chinese military strategies and Tai Chi

There are Chinese military strategy classics dating back to the 5th century BCE; the most famous is *The Art of War* by the strategist Sunzi. Tai Chi uses many of these strategies, such as 'retreat in order to advance' and 'now conceal, now reveal your intentions'. There were also many military training manuals, the best-known being *The Analytical New Book of General Qi Jiguang* (1528–87); this contains *The Classic of Boxing*, which had a profound effect on Tai Chi terminology.

Tai Chi only started to become famous around 1852, when Yang Luchan taught it in the Forbidden City to the Manchu Imperial Guard and to members of the imperial household. Outside his immediate family, his most successful Tai Chi disciples were the Wu family. Wu Quanyou was a Mongolian bannerman (professional soldier) in the Forbidden City and his son, Wu Jianquan, later spread the art throughout South-East Asia. Members of the Wu family served at the Nanjing Military Academy, training troops for the war against the Japanese during the Second World War.

Chinese martial arts and Tai Chi

Chinese martial arts, in the form of wrestling bouts, date back more than three thousand years: warriors needed to know how to fight both with and without weapons; sword dances were also performed from early times. The division of Chinese martial arts into hard/external and soft/internal dates only to a 1669 tombstone inscription of a Neijia Chuan/Internal Family Boxing master named Wang Zhengnan, which contrasted the approach of Internal Family Boxing and its founder (Zhang Sanfeng) with that of Shaolin, which relied on strength and was therefore considered external.

The other major Chinese internal martial arts are Baguazhang/'Eight Diagram Palm', which relies on circling, and Xingyi/'Form and Intent Boxing', which tends to be powerful and direct. Both have a similarity of terminology and approach with Tai Chi.

Tai Chi for all

Almost anyone can practise at least some aspects of Tai Chi. I have taught people affected by blindness and cerebral palsy, and those confined to wheelchairs; children of six and pensioners of 86. Tai Chi is infinitely adaptable.

The Chinese practise all aspects of Tai Chi outdoors, in all weathers and usually in the morning, though any time is fine. If you are going to practise it indoors, weapon practice will require a lot of space, whereas static meditation will not. Some modern Tai Chi forms are designed to be accompanied by music and many people enjoy practising it with music in the background, although it does affect your concentration.

Some Tai Chi schools insist that students wear traditional Tai Chi outfits, but for most people loose, casual clothing is fine. You can either be barefoot or wear soft shoes or socks. My Sifu sometimes practised in boxer shorts, and sometimes in a suit and tie while wearing Cuban heels.

Tai Chi styles

In a sense, everyone doing Tai Chi has his or her own style. However, there are two major lineages: Chen and Yang.

In the early 19th century a youth named Yang Luchan went to Chenjiagou/Chen-family village and learned Tai Chi from the master there, Chen Changxing. In 1852 Yang emerged from obscurity and taught Tai Chi in Beijing. He was nicknamed 'Invincible Yang' and made Tai Chi famous as a martial art. There is no record of the term Tai Chi Chuan before Yang's time, so it probably existed under another name.

Though there are differences in syllabus and technique, the basic Long Form sequence (see page 76) practised by most Tai Chi practitioners is derived from Yang Luchan. This sequence is very different from the one performed nowadays by the Chen family. Yang-lineage teachers generally claim the Taoist Zhang Sanfeng as their founder, while the Chens claim their ancestor Chen Wangting as their founder.

Why the differences in syllabus and technique and founder? The Chen village is near the famous Shaolin Temple and their family boxing, 'Cannon Punch', contains the technique 'Buddha's Warrior Attendant Pounds Mortar' – a definite Shaolin technique. In terms of the five major Tai Chi Classics (see page 231), only one verse of one Classic is part of the Chen syllabus. Furthermore, the Chens claim that their form originates wholly from the Chen family, yet it contains 29 of the 32 named techniques found in *The Classic of Boxing*, which is itself based on at least 16 different boxing systems – none of them being Chen.

The simplest explanation is that Tai Chi came to Chen village from outside, so there were two groups in the village: one practising Cannon Punch and the other practising Tai Chi. Over time the Chens became jealous of the success of the Yangs and so to reassert their position they blended Cannon Punch and Tai Chi, to create Chen Tai Chi and claimed it to be authentic and traditional. Chen-village forms and nearby Zhaobao-village forms are characterized by sudden changes of speed and a lot of gymnastic movement, which is similar in style to Shaolin boxing.

THE MAJOR YANG-LINEAGE STYLES ARE:

● Yang-family style, which is characterized by large, expansive movements. Cheng Man-ching style, which is more upright with smaller movements, is a variation of this. By all accounts the Yangs seem to have been peasants and are not credited with any major contributions to Tai Chi theory. However, they were the ones who first made Tai Chi famous and then popular.

● Wu style, of which I teach a variation; the movements are medium to large and the weight distribution is extreme compared to other styles. Wu Quanyou was a Mongolian bannerman who learned from Yang while serving in the Forbidden City. His son, Wu Jianquan, was a famous master, who taught my teacher's uncle. The Wu-style variation shown in this book, though technically similar to Wu-family Tai Chi, has a range of training methods that are not found in the family system or in other variations of Wu style. My teacher referred to his system as 'Wudang Tai Chi Chuan', tracing the origin back to Wudang Mountain and the Taoist recluse Zhang Sanfeng. The South-East Asian Chinese martial-arts fraternity coined the term 'Practical Tai Chi Chuan' to refer to it.

● Wu Yuxiang/Hao style, in which the movements are small and neat. Wu and his two brothers belonged to the gentry and wrote some essays on Tai Chi theory. They made connections for Yang Luchan in Beijing, which led to him being employed as a combat instructor in the Forbidden City.

● Sun style, which has small, neat movements as for Hao style (see above), but was also influenced by other methods of internal boxing. Its founder, Sun Lutang, also practised Baguazhang ('Eight Diagram Palm') and Xingyi ('Form and Intent Boxing'). He incorporated aspects of both into his Tai Chi.

Over the years many variations of all these styles have developed. Often family members have changed things rather more than loyal non-family students have.

Tai Chi and numerology

The Chinese are great mathematicians and numerologists, and numerology plays an important part in the theory and practice of Tai Chi. I have described some of the most significant numbers below.

● According to Chinese cosmology and the Tai Chi Classic *The Canon of Tai Chi Chuan*, Tai Chi ('Supreme Ultimate/Pole') was born of Wu Chi ('No Ultimate/Pole'). This concept is represented in Tai Chi form practice by the transition from the position Wu Chi/Tai Chi at rest to the position Tai Chi / Ready Style – from nothing to something. This is designed to focus mind and body for the form.

● In Chinese the number one is represented by a single horizontal line, which is said to represent the penis; all odd numbers are considered male. Two is represented by a pair of parallel horizontal lines, and even numbers are considered female.

● 'Embracing the One' is a Tai Chi Neigong technique and is a direct quotation from *The Classic of the Way and Virtue* by the Taoist philosopher Laozi (c. 5th century BCE); by this he meant the harmony of Heaven, Earth and Humanity so that they were as one. This is called Tao – 'the Way'. It is also the aim of Tai Chi practice and is represented at the beginning of the hand form by the 'Ready Style'.

● *The Canon of Tai Chi Chuan* goes on to say that Tai Chi is the mother of Yin and Yang and that 'in motion they separate, in stillness they combine'. Yin is depicted as a broken line, symbolizing the vagina, and represents the female, receptiveness, softness, night and negative values. Yang, like the number one, is depicted as an unbroken line and represents the male, penetration, hardness, day and positive values. 'Tai Chi in Harmony', at the end of the hand form, represents this combining in stillness.

- As well as representing the Taoist trinity of Heaven, Earth and Humanity, the number three represents the Three Treasures of Chinese internal alchemy. These are 'Qi' or vital force/energy (including the breath), 'Jing' or vital essence (body secretions) and 'Shen' or spiritual energy.

- There are 'Four Directions' (Peng, Lu, Ji, An) and 'Four Corners' (Cai, Lie, Zhou, Kao) pushing hands drills, which between them train the Eight Forces of Tai Chi.

- The Chinese concept of Five Elements is linked in the Classic work *The Tai Chi Chuan Discourse* to the concept of Five Steps: 'Step Forward, Move Back, Face Left, Look Right and Centrally Stable' are Metal, Wood, Water, Fire and Earth.

- There are Six Secret Words, each of them being a martial concept to be applied separately or jointly. They are normally taught to advanced students.

- 'Seven Stars'/'Seven Star Step' refers to the Northern Dipper, the abode of the god of longevity; this in turn is part of the Great Bear, the residence of Shangdi, the principal Taoist deity. The arm positions in these exercises are similar to the star configurations.

- According to Tai Chi theory, there are eight types of force to be used in bare-handed combat and pushing hands. Each of the weapons also has its own set of eight forces. The Eight Forces are identified with the Eight Trigrams, which are composed of combinations of broken and unbroken lines. They are identified with the eight directions. The *Tai Chi Chuan Discourse* states: 'Peng, Lu, Ji, An are the trigrams Qian, Kun, Kan, Li and are the four cardinal points. Cai, Lie, Zhou, Kao are the trigrams Sun, Chen, Tui, Kan, the four corners.' This concept of the Eight Forces and its link to the Eight Trigrams is somewhat artificial, but it has been adopted by every school of

Tai Chi. These Eight Forces are also mentioned in *The Fighter's Song*, though they are not explained there, either.

● The Eight Trigrams are depicted in a number of different arrangements in both Chinese philosophy and Taoist lore. The one referred to in this quotation is called 'Prior to Heaven' and is attributed to the legendary Emperor Fu Xi (c. 2400 BCE). As a rough guide, Peng (upward force) and Ji (forward directed force) go together and are at right-angles to one another in application. Lu (sideways diversion) and An (press down) also go together and are applied at right-angles to one another. Cai (uproot), Lie (spiral), Zhou (forearm) and Kao (shoulder and body) are seen as being applied diagonally (although in reality this is far from true).

● The pushing hand method 'Nine Palace Step' refers to the Altar of Nine Palaces found in Taoist temples, comprising the Eight Trigrams as the eight directions, with the Tai Chi as the centre. The concept is of both partners stepping into and out of the palaces.

● The 13 Tactics is an old name for Tai Chi; it comprises the Eight Forces and the Five Steps combined. The idea appears again in the name 'Eight Gates Five Steps', an alternative term for 'Four Corners'/'Dalu' pushing hands. In one of Tai Chi's many paradoxes, two of the Tai Chi Classics contain the term 13 Tactics in their titles, but fail to mention the 13 Tactics in the text.

The Eight Trigrams with the Tai Chi symbol in the centre making up the Nine Palaces

Chapter 1

Wisdom LEARNING HOW TO USE TAI CHI

Meditation

Many people think of Tai Chi as some kind of meditation, but before looking at specific links between Tai Chi and meditation, let's look at the mechanics of meditation.

According to Webster's *Third New International Dictionary*, meditation is, or can be, 'steady or close meditative reflection: continued application of the mind'; or 'a private devotion or spiritual exercise consisting of deep, continued reflection on a religious theme'; or 'spoken or written discourse treated in a contemplative manner and intended to express its author's reflections or to guide others in contemplation'. Tai Chi embraces all of these definitions to a greater or lesser degree. Taoistic practices include meditation, therapeutic and hygienic exercise and martial arts, and of all these separate aspects can be found in Tai Chi.

What are we trying to achieve through meditation, and how can we realize such achievements? Often there is some kind of ritual involved – before, during and after meditation; is this an essential element and, if so, why? Many Samurai (members of the military class in feudal Japan) practised Zen to help them become calm and spontaneous in a combat situation. The softer aspects of Tai Chi have a similar function. Ritual acts as a trigger to prepare the body and mind for the meditation journey

Where should you do your meditation: outdoors or indoors? If you meditate outside, then the time of day is relevant. The Chinese commonly practise Tai Chi forms in the early morning, because that is when trees and plants give out oxygen; there are also fewer people around at that time, and Tai Chi readies the practitioner for the day ahead. In many parts of China the summer months are hot and humid, making it unpleasant to practise during the day, so dawn and, to a lesser degree, dusk are the preferred times. If you are practising a traditional Tai Chi Long Form outdoors in the morning, then it is best to start off facing west, so that the sun will be in your face for a minimal amount of time.

If you are practising a more static form of meditation, then you are more likely to be disturbed by the wind, sun and other elements, and even by birds and animals. That is why many Taoists and hermits – such as Zhang Sanfeng on Wudang Mountain and in Bao Ji, and Bodhidharma on Songshan – are reputed to have practised in caves. Caves were common dwelling places of wild animals, so they were seen as places with very powerful Qi.

Meditation was particularly linked in Chinese society with Taoist and Buddhist religious communities. Some temples and monasteries were deliberately located in remote areas such as mountains and were specifically designed internally for meditation and contemplation.

Whether religious or not, meditation often involves chanting and the repetition of mantras (spoken words or sounds). The Tai Chi Classics are mnemonic in nature – that is, they are designed to be chanted as an aid to learning. They are contemplative, they express their authors' reflections and they act as guides to others on how better to perform Tai Chi. Many of my students listen to a CD of the Classics while practising, or even when in repose.

圖面正功內

Tai Chi initially involves training the body in movement by learning postures, exercises, forms and drills; through this you learn to focus the mind and develop intent. Focusing is necessary for effective practice of most aspects of the art. Next comes coordination of the external postures and movements with the internal, to develop and control Qi, Jing and Shen (or, in Western terms, respiration and circulation, vitality and spirit); it is also necessary to develop internal force. Finally there is the ultimate Taoist (and therefore Tai Chi) goal of becoming empty – that is, free of ego and delusion – so that one can merge with the Tao; this can also be considered to be the attainment of 'No Mind', when the ancient Taoist trinity of Heaven, Earth and Humanity unites harmoniously as one, the Tao itself. My teacher often referred to Tai Chi as a means to 'Receive the Way', where we (as Humanity, composed of Yin and Yang) are rooted (usually by our feet) to the Supreme Yin of Earth and, with Shen (spiritual energy) rising to the top of the head, aspire to the Supreme Yang of Heaven.

Five of the static Neigong exercises are done with the eyes shut and so are partly meditational, although they all have other functions. Practising Tai Chi forms with the eyes closed is likewise a way of sharpening the other senses. You have to feel your foot positions on the floor and orient yourself according to any ambient sounds or vibrations, while visualizing the performance of the exercises or forms.

In certain professions getting to sleep is a real problem. Many years ago one of my new students, who had been practising Yang-style Tai Chi for some years, told me that as a printer he worked irregular hours and had to have expensive acupuncture treatment once every couple of weeks to help him sleep. I taught him only the first four Yin exercises of Tai Chi Neigong and he had no further problems. Shift workers, including police officers whom I have taught, have reported similar benefits.

In Tai Chi, whether in meditation or otherwise, the breathing should be deep when you inhale and long when you exhale; it should be slow, continuous and

Taoist Neigong meditational posture

almost imperceptible. Many types of Chinese meditation are preceded by breathing exercises – as is the case with the final Tai Chi Neigong exercise. There is an emphasis on abdominal respiration so that the lungs expand more fully than usual, thus taking in more oxygen, which makes the circulation and purification of the blood more effective. In turn, a higher percentage of carbon dioxide is breathed out, or methane gas emitted.

This relates to enhancing the development of the Three Treasures of Qi, Jing and Shen (see page 244). Qi vitalizes the body, while Jing in the form of semen, saliva and bodily secretions irrigates it; Shen was developed by the Yin-Yang method of closing or shutting out the exterior world of the senses and the interior world of thought and emotions (which are, of course, affected by the outer world), while opening ourselves to the spiritual world of the infinite.

Some people say the longer your meditation practice the better and recommend a minimum of 30 minutes. I have practised Tai Chi nearly every day since 1975, but when I do Neigong sitting meditation it is rarely for more than ten minutes. Maybe this is because of the significant amount of Tai Chi practice that I do – indeed, many forms of Taoist meditation are preceded by massage or stretching exercises, which mentally and physically prepare the adept. I strongly believe that long practice of sitting meditation can be bad for you, leading to drowsiness and lassitude, as well as sometimes damaging the knees by cutting off the circulation.

It is clear that some aspects of Tai Chi – in particular the solo practice of forms and Neigong – do have a meditative element, although they are not solely meditative. However, you will only benefit from meditation and from Tai Chi if you have the appropriate attitude and lifestyle, and if you find a suitable teacher.

Reclining Tiger Qigong posture

卧虎撲食勢

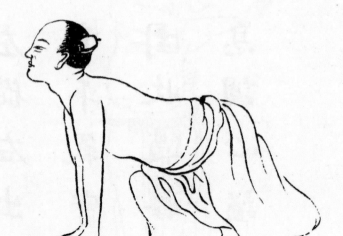

Neigong

In Chinese hygienic exercise and martial arts there are hundreds of different Qigong and Neigong systems. Some are meditative, others therapeutic; some are martial, others train internal alchemy. Some, like Tai Chi Neigong, contain all these elements. Others are even dangerous and can cause both psychological and physical trauma. This is well documented and I have witnessed such cases myself. The Chinese refer to this phenomenon as 'Walk fire, enter demon'.

In the 1970s I had a much older Tai Chi brother called Mr Shum, who was a businessman. One day his anxious wife brought him to my Sifu's studio. Elder Brother told Sifu that he felt his Qi was stuck and could not go up or down. He felt that he wanted to fly – a dangerous wish in high-rise Hong Kong. Elder Brother was also ejaculating spontaneously at business meetings. Elder Brother was not okay. Sifu asked him if he had been doing internal-alchemy Qigong. Elder Brother said that he had done some with a Sifu from China. It took three days to cure him. Qigong and Neigong systems directly affect the nervous system, so finding an experienced teacher with a proven method is essential.

There are two old Chinese martial-arts sayings: 'Two hands cannot deal with four' and 'If you learn the boxing [Chuan] but don't practise the Gong [conditioning such as the 24 Tai Chi Neigong exercises], even if you train till you are old, it is still empty.' Although a large number of Tai Chi techniques are designed for use against two or more opponents, you are more likely to be hit if you are fighting more than one adversary. And you may know all the techniques, but if you lack the ability to apply them effectively, they are useless.

Neigong (sometimes called internal strength) is part of an oral or 'inside the door' tradition; students who have already been training for some time, and who have shown commitment, go through a ceremony of discipleship before they start to practise it. It was taught sparingly. My teacher's uncle failed to complete the training, though he became a famous master of Tai Chi in Hong Kong, so my Sifu had to go elsewhere to receive a complete transmission of the art. Most Tai Chi practitioners have never heard of Neigong and even among those who have (including those who have learned it), very few actually practise it. Neigong training is time-consuming and arduous.

Many years ago a rich Tai Chi fan in her sixties asked my Sifu if he would teach her Neigong. Having an old-fashioned attitude towards women, he said that she could do the ceremony of discipleship with him and would be able to call him her Sifu, but he would not actually show her the exercises himself and instead would ask one of his students to do this. He also asked her for a lot of money. She refused his conditions, telling us later that she would have been happy to pay a lot more, but was not willing to be shown the exercises by a mediocre student. When I visited Hong Kong the next year she asked me to teach her. I realized that her main motivation was to gain prestige among her Tai Chi friends, but as she had always treated me well, I agreed to teach her. She paid me the same amount that my Sifu had asked for.

Neigong practice is more important than form practice. By the way, *Gong* is the same character as the *Kung* in Kung Fu (which means 'skill acquired through effort'; it is not a term restricted to martial arts). The static postures are held for long periods, while the moving techniques are practised dozens, or even hundreds, of times. This builds a strong muscle memory and as 16 of the techniques have martial applications, these will become those that you are most likely to use in self-defence. Through training, techniques become more refined and focused, and the body is strengthened and able to withstand blows from an opponent.

Women who practise Tai Chi can do all that men can do, and often do it better. However, Neigong practice sometimes affects the menstrual cycle. I have taught Neigong to hundreds of ladies and every one is different. Some choose to stop Neigong practice several days before menstruation and wait to resume it until several days after it ends, because doing Neigong during the cycle – though not dangerous – can make it more unpleasant than usual. Other ladies are able to train right through it with no problem. Still others even find that Neigong causes menstruation to cease.

Neigong in Action

Warning!

This illustration of Neigong in action
was performed by highly experienced
Tai Chi practitioners, and should not be
attempted by readers.

3

Basic Stances

FRONT/BOW STANCE

The 'Front Stance' is so called because the body is inclined forward, putting most of the weight on the front foot; it is also called the 'Bow Stance' because the front leg is bent like a bow, but the front knee should not go beyond the toes, as this damages the knee joint. The stance is held for as long as is comfortable. In the hand form, sabre form and sword form the feet are normally shoulder-width apart, but in the spear form the stance is a bit narrower. The back foot is turned in and, with certain techniques (like 'Step Back and Repulse Monkey'), the feet are parallel.

BACK STANCE

The 'Back Stance' is so called because the body is erect, putting most of the weight on the back foot, while the front foot rests on the heel. The stance is held for as long as is comfortable and the feet are normally shoulder-width apart. The back foot is turned in and, with certain techniques (like 'Brush Knee Twist Step'), the feet are parallel, but the back knee should not go beyond the toes, as this damages the knee joint.

CAT STANCE

The 'Cat Stance' is so called because one foot is on tiptoe, like a cat. The front cat stance is similar to the 'Back Stance' (see previous page): the back is straight, but the body is not always erect; most of the weight is on the back foot, while the front foot is on tiptoe.

REVERSE CAT STANCE

The 'Reverse Cat Stance' is similar to the front 'Cat Stance', but it is the rear foot that is on tiptoe. The stance is held for as long as is comfortable and the feet are normally shoulder-width apart in forms ('Seven Star Step' is a bit different). The back foot is turned in.

HORSE-RIDING STANCE

In the 'Horse-Riding Stance' the heels are one-and-a-half to two shoulder-widths apart and the toes are slightly turned out. The weight is on the heels and on the outside of the feet and is evenly distributed. There is a straight line between the crown of the head and the tailbone. The knees should not go beyond the toes, as this damages the knee joint.

Tai Chi in application

Sanshou/Scattering Hands is what the Chinese call self-defence. A comparison of the list of 48 Sanshou techniques with the list of Long Form techniques in the system that I teach reveals that only four of the techniques are not found in the form. Of the form techniques, most have multiple applications and many have a number of variations, each reflecting a different method of application. For example, there are four variations of 'Flying Oblique'; four different versions of 'Brush Knee Twist Step'; and so on.

The late, great Hong Kong master of Wing-Chun boxing and street-fighting Bruce Lee mentor, Wong Shun-leung, once said to me that the most important form techniques were those that occur most often in a form. Looking at the Long Form, we can see that 'Seven Stars', 'Grasping the Bird's Tail' and 'Single Whip' (a particularly complex and versatile technique) fall into this category. It follows that those interested in Tai Chi as a martial art should spend more time in training the application of these techniques. The same applies to applications of weapon-form techniques.

Some Tai Chi techniques are deliberately designed for use against specific techniques from other martial arts. For example, 'As if Shutting a Door' is perfect for dealing with chain punches, while 'Grasping the Bird's Tail' is effective against the heavy swing-punches employed by many hard styles.

Throwing techniques are effective because most people don't know how to fall and they are particularly efficacious when taking advantage of the opponent's attacking momentum. As far as strikes are concerned, we use our hands to hit the head, neck and torso down to the groin; we use our feet and knees to strike targets from the waist to the foot. As a police officer, I found the holds and locks very useful in controlling and restraining arrested persons. Some Tai Chi techniques (in particular those from the Neigong exercises) target pressure points and this is often regarded as a secret art. It is not; most people simply lack the skill to be able to perform it.

The Long Form and weapon forms are important sources of techniques and sequences that are designed to be used against multiple opponents, or in combination against a single assailant. All techniques should be used with discrimination, according to the particular situation. Some are more appropriate against a taller opponent, others against a smaller person. Equally, some techniques are easier for a tall person to apply, and others are easier for a smaller person. I once knocked out a 160-kg (350-lb) fighter from Five Ancestor Boxing in Malaysia; I never considered trying to throw him ...

Many Tai Chi schools try to teach the application of techniques exactly as they appear in the form; there is no evasion, no footwork. This is car-crash Tai Chi. Such schools and their adepts have rightly earned the contempt of the martial-arts world. So if the forms and Neigong practice aren't sufficient to train footwork and evasion, what does achieve this?

The role of pushing hands

Tuishou, or pushing hands, is a core part of the Tai Chi syllabus, although it involves more than just pushing and the use of the hands. It is the Tai Chi method of teaching us to deal with an opponent at close quarters, by neutralizing and controlling his or her movements and unbalancing him or her. This method includes many drills as well as free pushing, where each person tries to unbalance the other. Steps can be fixed, restricted or moving.

An old name for Tai Chi is the 13 Tactics (Shisanshi), comprising the Eight Forces of upward diversion (Peng), sideways diversion (Lu), push upward (Ji), press down (An), uproot (Cai), spiral (Lie), forearm (Zhou) and barge (Kao), plus the Five Steps of forward, back, left, right and central equilibrium. Pushing hands is an ideal method of practising the 13 Tactics with a partner.

Pushing hands with a partner trains distance, timing, balance, coordination and the effective use of skilled force in both attack and defence. 'Seven Star Step' trains diagonal side-steps, forward and back; it can be used either defensively or offensively. 'Nine Palace Step' uses the cross-step, either as evasion or to spin (spinning is particularly useful when applying Sword and Sabre techniques and/or when dealing with more than one opponent) and strike/lock the opponent. 'Four Corners' pushing hands is an advanced method of stepping forward and back while remaining connected to the opponent. 'Bow Down, Look Up' pushing hands trains us to bend and sway out of range of attacks, in situations where we cannot move our feet.

The Canon of Tai Chi Chuan states, 'By practice and familiarity, we gradually come to understand force. By understanding force, we can achieve enlightenment. However, we must be diligent over a long period of time and can't suddenly become expert.' Pushing hands also trains us in understanding Jin – skilful force. This is a three-step process involving Ting Jin (listening for Jin), Hua Jin (using Jin to redirect the opponent's Jin) and Fa Jin (discharging Jin by applying the Eight Forces through pushing, pressing, pulling, neutralizing, diverting, spiralling and using the forearm or shoulder). You and your partner/opponent may use one or both hands and may simultaneously practise a wide variety of footwork or practise on the spot. The key is to 'listen' to what your partner is doing and respond instantly, by redirecting his or her force and discharging your own force. The ability to understand force is not only important in pushing hands, but is also vital in all bare-handed and weapon applications.

Skill in pushing hands is not an end in itself, although for many Tai Chi practitioners this is what it has become.

Eight Forces

Peng UPWARD FORCE

1

Ji DIRECT FORWARD FORCE

2

Lu SIDEWAYS DIVERSION

①

An PRESSING FORCE

2

Cai UPROOTING

Lie SPIRALLING FORCE

Zhou FOREARM

Kao BARGE

Five strategies

In *The Fighter's Song* we read, 'Adhere, be continuous, be soft, follow, don't break contact or resist' and this five-step strategy is applied by Tai Chi practitioners in pushing hands and close-distance combat.

First, to be able to listen to or feel your opponent's force, your arms need to stick to your opponent's arms. Second, you should be continuous in your actions and not jerky; defence and counter are as one. Third, if you are stiff you cannot listen effectively, so your arms need to be soft like cotton. Fourth, you should follow and not resist your opponent's movements; if he steps forward, you step back and vice versa. Lastly, don't lose contact with your partner and don't use force against force. Once you lose contact with your opponent, you cannot feel what he is doing and it immediately becomes a potential hitting situation for both of you. Using force against force is crude, and a waste of energy; it is a higher skill to change from hard to soft than from soft to hard. From a martial point of view, a fight may start off from a distance, but as soon as there is contact, pushing hands skills come into play.

The Canon of Tai Chi Chuan states, 'Follow, bending then straightening. When the opponent is hard and stiff and I am pliant and soft, this is called moving. When I am smooth and the opponent is not, this is called adherence.'

Free pushing hands

Pushing hands training can take the form of drills or it can be freer, where the object may be to unbalance, throw, sweep or even strike your opponent. There are well-established pushing hands competitions in many countries. It is advisable to be clear about the rules before agreeing to push hands with someone new. I once pushed hands with a large and rough fellow, who hit me in the face after I had unbalanced him. He immediately said, 'Sorry, natural reaction.' I said, 'No problem.' We continued. I trapped his arm and hit hard on his elbow joint. He collapsed and swore at me. I said, 'Sorry, natural reaction.'

At the other end of the spectrum, many people when pushing hands are trying to *feel* something (the term 'energy' is often used, but rarely defined) instead of trying to *do* something; it is dull to push with these types. On one visit to Hong Kong I was asked to do a pushing hands demonstration. My Sifu gave me a senior Chinese female student as a partner. She told me that she had a teaching certificate for pushing hands, so we started to push and I began to introduce foot-sweeps and spirals. She was nonplussed and said that she had never done such techniques before. We went to see my Sifu, who confirmed that she had a certificate to teach pushing hands – for health. She could do the drills, but had no idea how to apply them practically.

In the end the best reason for practising free pushing hands is that it can be a lot of fun, as well as teaching you about balance and timing.

Pushing hands drills and skills

SEVEN STAR STEP

This is the first thing I teach new students. It can be done as a solo exercise or with a partner.

Start without a partner, standing with your feet apart. Step diagonally forward with the left foot, with the right foot following it, into a 'Reverse Cat Stance' (see page 41), pushing out with the right palm and turning the body, with the left hand under the chin. Now step diagonally forward with the right foot, with the left foot following it, into a 'Reverse Cat Stance', pushing out with the left palm, with the right hand under the chin. Continue until you have stepped forward and pushed seven times.

Now step diagonally back with the right foot, with the left foot following it, into a 'Front Cat Stance' (see page 40). At the same time turn the body to the right and bring the arms across to the right: left palm down, right palm up. Continue until you have stepped back and diverted across seven times.

To do it with a partner, you should both stand with your feet apart. As one person steps diagonally forward with the left foot and pushes with the right hand, the other person steps back diagonally with the right foot, turning the body to the right and bringing the arms across to the right: left palm down on the elbow of the pushing arm, right hand palm up on the wrist of the pushing arm. Match one another's movements like this in one direction; once you have done seven pushes matched by seven diversions, change roles and go zigzagging back the other way.

This drill trains balance, coordination and footwork and, when done with a partner, it also trains timing, distance, evasion and interception. There are a number of possible variations to the drill, which should be done briskly, once you are familiar with it.

I was once attacked at a party as I came out of the toilet. I side-stepped with 'Seven Star Step' and my assailant went crashing through the toilet door. His need must have been great, for he took quite some time to return.

Seven Star Step

SOLO

Seven Star Step

PAIR

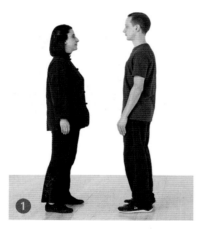

Bow Down, Look Up
FU YANG

This is a simple and useful drill for the whole body. Face your partner, both of you with the same foot forward. As your partner pushes your shoulders back, bend back to absorb the force and place your hands on top of your partner's hands to retain your balance. Your partner is now bowing down, while you are looking up. At all times maintain hand contact.

As your partner brings his hands down your body, continue to observe his pressure, bending in at the waist when his hands reach that level. When his hands reach your knees, your partner should bring your hands onto his shoulders and you should take your turn to press, while he absorbs. When pushing, the weight is forward; when absorbing, the weight is back.

This drill involves flexibility and stretching. It should be performed slowly, changing feet from time to time. The aim is not just to absorb the push, but also to train you to bend and sway, to avoid attacks such as punches and kicks.

1

Reeling Silk
CHAN SI

In this drill the arms stay in contact and circle smoothly, as if reeling silk from a cocoon. Sometimes your arms should be on top; sometimes your partner's arms should be on top. Maintaining arm contact, you can step back and forward.

The object is to try and strike one another with the palm or back of the hand and to use your listening skills and neutralize your partner's attempted strikes. This is useful training for Sanshou techniques such as 'Gyrating Arms' and 'Flying Flower Palm'.

Nine Palace Step
SOLO

Try this first without a partner, left foot forward. Step across with the front foot and push with the left hand. Hand and foot should both point forward; the other hand should be under the chin. Step across with the right foot and push with the right hand. Now step across to the left with the left foot, shifting the weight

back. At the same time turn the body to the right, bringing the arms across to the right: right hand palm up, left hand palm down. Now step back with the right foot, shifting the weight back. At the same time turn the body to the left, bringing the arms across to the left: left hand palm up, right hand palm down. Your feet have walked a diamond or cross shape.

With a partner, you should both start with the left foot forward and the left wrists in contact. Step across with the front foot and push with the left hand; your partner should shift his weight back and divert your push to his left: with his left hand palm up and controlling your wrist, his right hand palm down and controlling your elbow. Now step across with the right foot and push with the right hand: your partner should step back with his left foot and divert your push to his right, with his right hand palm up and controlling your wrist, his left hand palm down and controlling your elbow. Now it is his turn to give two pushes, and your turn to divert them ... and so on.

In the beginning, the arm movements are linear, but later they are rounded into two intersecting circles, which express the forces Peng, Lu, Ji, An. There are also foot and arm variations.

As with 'Seven Star Step', this drill trains balance, coordination and footwork (especially the cross-step) and, when done with a partner, also trains timing, distance, evasion, spinning and interception. The drill should be done briskly, once you are familiar with it. Using the cross-step with a spin is particularly handy when dealing with more than one opponent, or when training weapon applications.

Nine Palace Step
PAIR

Four Directions

SOLO

In this drill the arm movements are the same as in 'Nine Palace Step' (see pages 68–71), but instead of side-stepping, you shift the weight forward when you push and shift it back when you divert. This is the most versatile of pushing hand drills, having multiple variations and applications, including stepping back and forward, using sweeps, locks and kicks.

1

Four Directions

PAIR

Chapter 2

48 Forms

Revelations

TECHNIQUES IN FORM AND APPLICATION

The 48 techniques shown in this chapter appear in the sequence (with all repetitions omitted) in the Long Form that I teach. For each technique, a practical description is followed by an indication of the physical and health benefits that are linked to it. Wherever possible, an explanation of the background to the technique name is given. Where relevant, the martial applications are provided, to show potential ways of using each technique. Finally, top tips are given for each technique.

One of the unanswered, and unanswerable, questions about Tai Chi is to what extent the art – particularly the Long Form – has been influenced by *The Classic of Boxing*, which is attributed to General Qi Jiguang (1528–87). Where names of techniques appear both in *The Classic of Boxing* and in the Long Form, a separate box provides the quotation and indicates possible connections. A detailed treatment of *The Classic of Boxing* can be found in my book *Tai Chi Chuan: Decoding the Classics for the Modern Martial Artist*.

All form moves and their application should be practised for a few minutes each, to achieve any benefit. Note that in most cases there are many more applications than the one shown. Many techniques are designed to be used against specific attacks from other styles. Although techniques are shown on one side of the body only, in form and in application they should be practised on both sides.

1 Wu Chi/Tai Chi at Rest

DESCRIPTION

This is normally a preparatory position prior to doing the form. The feet are shoulder-width apart and slightly turned out. The palms are parallel to the ground. The feet should feel rooted to the ground; the spine should be erect. Wu Chi can also be a meditation position, with the eyes closed, to train your balance.

BACKGROUND

Wu Chi means 'No Ultimate/Pole' – the situation that gives birth to Tai Chi. Although you are not yet ready to do Tai Chi, you stop doing whatever else you were doing.

TOP TIP
Don't stiffen the hands.

2 Tai Chi/Ready Style

DESCRIPTION

This preparatory position is the same
as Wu Chi, except that the fingers
now point down. Try closing the eyes
and visualizing the form while in
this position.

BACKGROUND

As in philosophy, so in form; Wu Chi gives
birth to Tai Chi. In both a physical and a
psychological sense, you switch on.

TOP TIP
Look straight ahead with
neutral focus.

3 Beginning Style

DESCRIPTION

Slowly raise the arms to shoulder height, bending them and inhaling as you bring them in towards the body; at the same time open the rib cage. Bend the knees, sink, exhale, close the ribcage and lower the arms. The hands are soft at all times, as if swimming in the air.

This move flexes the joints, stretches the lungs and promotes circulation.

TOP TIP
Keep the hands soft.

MARTIAL APPLICATION

As the opponent steps in to grab your neck, you should step back, raising the arms, palms cupped. Then suddenly step forward, trapping his front foot, and push/palm-strike him with both hands.

4 Vanguard Arms and Extend Arms

DESCRIPTION

Bring the arms up to shoulder level and step forward with the left foot. As you bring the arms in towards the centre, turn the left foot in. Bring the hands up in front of the chest, palm facing palm, and shift your weight at the same time onto the left foot. Incline your body weight forward, into the technique.

This strengthens the spine and the limbs.

TOP TIP
Keep the hands aero-dynamic in shape.

MARTIAL APPLICATION

Side-step and intercept the opponent's head punch. Sweep/trip his front leg with your left foot, simultaneously slapping him in the kidney and the face.

5 Seven Stars Style

DESCRIPTION

The stars are represented by the shoulders, elbows and wrists, and by the fingertips of the front hand. Turn right by pivoting on the ball of the rear foot, simultaneously reaching over with the right hand.

This trains spinal rotation and focus. Some styles call this position 'Stroke the Lute'; indeed, the two techniques are very similar.

TOP TIP
Minimize arm movement when turning.

MARTIAL APPLICATION

Face the opponent with your fingers, nose and front foot pointed towards him. This is the basic on-guard position in Tai Chi.

BACKGROUND

The seven stars referred to are those of the Northern Dipper, and the arm positions trace out the configuration of the stars.

Connections with
The Classic of Boxing

There is also a 'Seven Stars Fists' technique in *The Classic of Boxing*, with the arms crossed, as in the Tai Chi technique 'Step up Seven Stars'. Please note these techniques are not the same as the 'Seven Star Step' pushing hands drill.

6 Grasping the Bird's Tail

DESCRIPTION

In this technique you use the forces Peng, Lu, Ji, An, Ji. From 'Seven Stars', bring the body and arms around to the right, turning both arms as you bring them under, and then up to the right as you step forward onto the right foot. This is Peng. Turn the body right and start to bring the weight back, turning the arms. This is Lu. Bring the hands in to the left hip. This is An. Shift the weight

forward and push out at 45 degrees with the right palm. This is Ji.

This move flexes the limbs and the centre line.

TOP TIP

Coordinate the arm movement with shifting your weight and turning the body.

MARTIAL APPLICATION

High: Lift and twist the arm (Peng) to deflect the opponent's swing to the head; use the other hand to jam (An) his other arm. Palm-strike (Ji) him.

Connections with *The Classic of Boxing*

The name of the first technique in *The Classic of Boxing*, 'Lazily Tying Clothes', sounds the same as 'Grasping Bird's Tail' in Chinese, so there may be a connection, although this is another Tai Chi mystery.

Gesture 1:
'Lazily Tying Clothes' is the going out the door (beginning) technique.

Change to Low/Next technique (this could be a reference to 'Snake Creeps Down'); quick-steps Single Whip. Face the enemy as if afraid of nothing and go forward. Empty yourself, eyes clear and hands ready.'

Low: Bring the arm down and twist it to deflect (Lu) an attack to the body. At the same time jam his other arm. Palm-strike his face.

7 Single Whip

DESCRIPTION

Keeping the right arm extended, turn the body and turn the front foot in slightly, bringing the right arm around to the left in an arc, at the end of which the right hand forms a hook. Step across with the left foot into a 'Horse-Riding Stance'. Bring the left hand across, palm facing in. As it passes the body, turn the left hand, then push out and sink.

'Single Whip' is one of the techniques common to all Tai Chi Chuan styles that I am aware of, though there are considerable variations in execution. In the Wu Quan-you lineage, to which I belong in part, the technique is executed in a 'Horse-Riding Stance' when it is performed in hand form. It is also one of the most repeated techniques in the Long Form, occurring more than ten times in the form I practise, which gives a hint as to its relative importance.

When talking of 'Single Whip', many exponents tend to think of the completed position, but at its most sophisticated there is much coiling and uncoiling of arms, legs and torso before arriving at that point.

There are suggestions that there was also a 'Double Whip', and this is likely, as we have 'Single' and 'Double Seize Leg' and 'Single' and 'Double Sweep Lotus Leg'. There is also the idea that the body is the stock of the whip and the arms the lash. 'Single Whip' also exists in external arts such as Changquan, where it ends in a front stance with the fists extended. In addition there is the little-known Tai Chi Bian or 'Whip', which is a rattan cane, and it is possible (as in the Filipino martial art of Escrima) that

'Single Whip' referred to holding one of these while doing the same movements, while 'Double Whip' referred to using one stick/*bian* in each hand.

There is also the idea that the hooked hand is brandishing a whip, as if on horseback (the Wu family were descended from Manchu bannermen and were renowned horsemen). Other reasons for the 'Horse-Riding Stance' include leg-strengthening and stimulation of the autonomic nervous system.

TOP TIP

In horse-riding stance the feet are turned out and the weight is on the heels and the outer edge of the foot.

MARTIAL APPLICATION

There are multiple applications for 'Single Whip'. Here you intercept and control the opponent's back fist, at the same time stepping to the side and palming his head with the other hand.

The application shown for the next technique, 'Flying Oblique', is like a follow-up to 'Single Whip'. This linking in application of separate but consecutive techniques is common in Tai Chi.

Connections with *The Classic of Boxing*

'Single Whip' is the fourth of 32 techniques in *The Classic of Boxing*.

Gesture 4:
'Bent Single Whip, Yellow Flower advances urgently (yellow flower is a metaphor for a virgin, so step like a virgin with closed legs when you advance).

Open and lift his legs, left and right, it is difficult for him to defend. Snatch step (lunge step, as in fencing) and use the fist continuously to chop (with a hammer fist) the front. Chen Xiang gesture/style, push over Tai Shan' (Chen Xiang's mother had the sacred mountain of Taishan put on top of her and he lifted it off, thus saving her life).

8 Flying Oblique

DESCRIPTION

'Flying Oblique' can be low or high. Here we show the high position. Twist the body to the left, bringing the hands into the chest in anti-clockwise circles, then pivot on the right foot and shift the weight onto the left foot, extending the arms.

This technique manipulates the limbs and spine. If you hold the final position, it also stimulates the heart and circulation through the force of gravity.

TOP TIP
The arms are gently rounded in shape, but not bent.

MARTIAL APPLICATION

In application the left arm can be used
to lock the opponent's neck after 'Single
Whip', while the other hand strikes his
exposed torso.

9 Single and Double Hand Seize Legs

DESCRIPTION

These are two Inner Form techniques, and their names are not to be found in Tai Chi books. They are usually included as part of the next technique, 'Raise Hands Step Up'. Step up with the right foot, at the same time drawing two pairs of intersecting circles with the arms. These techniques work on the limbs and spine, while gravity works on the circulation in the arms.

TOP TIP
Make sure you turn the body when drawing the two circles.

MARTIAL APPLICATION

'Single Hand Seize Leg' can be used against a roundhouse (hook) kick, with one arm catching and flipping the kicking leg, while the other hand strikes and presses on the opponent's head. In effect we are using circular force.

I used 'Double Hand Seize Legs' while fighting Chinese full-contact against a Chikechuan stylist in Singapore in 1976. I ducked under a hook, seized his legs and hit him with my shoulder to throw him. Perfect Double Hands Seize Legs.

1

2

10 Raise Hands Step Up

DESCRIPTION

From 'Double Hand Seize Legs', in a crouched position, with palm facing palm in front of the chest, straighten both legs and both arms (one up, one down) simultaneously.

This technique stretches the whole body, including the lungs.

TOP TIP

The right arm should twist as you raise it.

MARTIAL APPLICATION

This is used to duck under and intercept a punch to the head. As you grab the opponent's wrist you strike to the groin, pulling and lifting, to throw him over your shoulder.

11 White Crane Flaps its Wings

DESCRIPTION

Keeping the arms in position, bend forward until the torso is more or less parallel to the ground and turn the body to the left.

This realigns the spinal column and promotes abdominal breathing.

TOP TIP
Keep the back straight and don't bend the knees.

MARTIAL APPLICATION

Step inside and intercept the opponent's swing punch and jam his other arm, then step in, grabbing him and pivoting as you throw him over your hip.

12 Break Arm Style

DESCRIPTION

This is another Inner Form technique, usually considered part of 'White Crane Flaps its Wings'. Raise the left arm and the torso as you turn right, bringing both hands across, high and to the right, then down, while sinking at the same time.

This technique twists and coils the whole body, while also working on the circulation.

TOP TIP
Let the body movement lead the arm movement.

MARTIAL APPLICATION

After parrying the opponent's swing punch to the body, step in, coiling your parrying arm under his, to put him in a shoulder lock.

13 Brush Knee Twist Step

DESCRIPTION

Continue the last movement, sweeping the arms out to the left, stepping out onto the left heel; the left arm draws a large clockwise circle in front of the body, while the right draws an anti-clockwise circle to the right. As the right hand finishes its circle with a palm strike, the left hand comes to rest on the outside of the left knee.

Twisting the centre line (spine) and the arms and legs prior to delivering the palm strike manipulates the joints and tendons, making them more flexible and stimulating the blood supply.

1

TOP TIP

Make sure that the weight goes forward with the palm strike, and not before.

MARTIAL APPLICATION

'Brush Knee Twist Step' is one of the most-repeated, and therefore one of the most important, techniques in Yang-lineage Long Forms. There are a number of variations of the technique in these Long Forms, including doing it after performing a 180-degree turn; this last represents a defence against an attack from behind.

Many years ago an old student of mine, Tebo Steele, used this technique to good effect against a kick-boxer in a Chinese full-contact contest. Tebo caught a kick with his left arm and hit the kick-boxer in the face with the other hand, knocking him out. Classical Tai Chi.

BACKGROUND

'Brush Knee Twist Step' is so called because in application you brush aside the opponent's kick, or catch it in a scooping action with the wrist or elbow joint of your front arm, while giving him a palm strike with your other hand, thus twisting his step and causing him to fall. This would normally be done with a side-step – a movement absent from the form. The transfer forward of the body weight and the palm strike must be coordinated; the finished hand positions are said to resemble the paddling flippers of a terrapin.

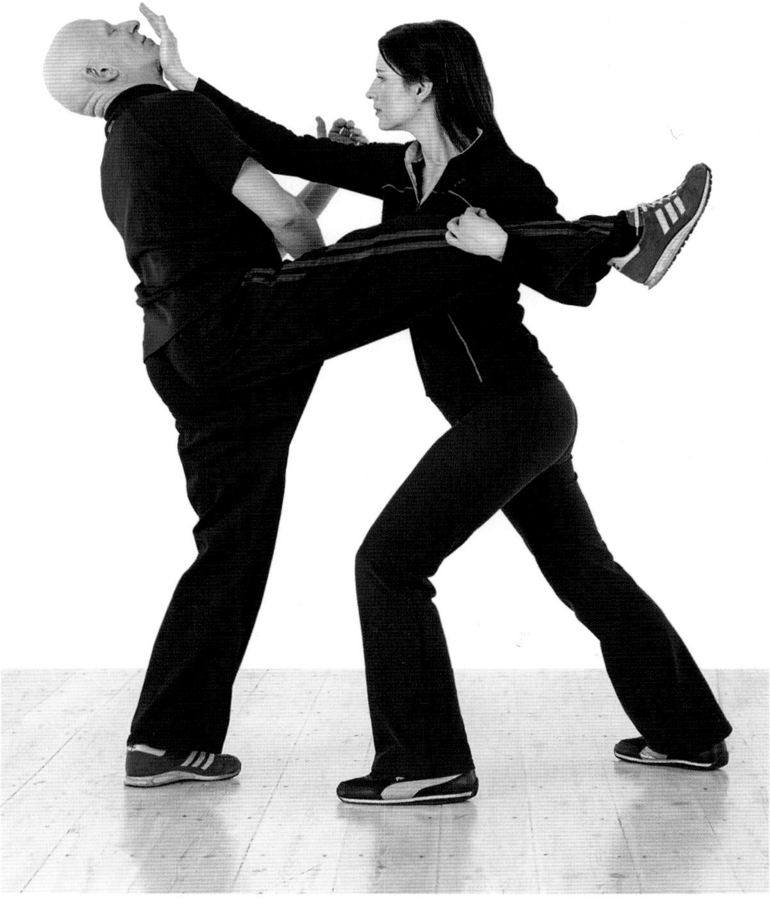

14 Stroke the Lute

DESCRIPTION

Step onto the left heel with the left hand forward, in the 'Seven Stars' position, then flatten the hands, drawing an anti-clockwise circle to the left, and bring the weight forward. Draw another circle as you step up with the back foot so that the feet are shoulder-width apart; the hands should end up in front of the waist.

This technique flexes the limbs and spine.

TOP TIP
Don't splay the fingers.

MARTIAL APPLICATION

The opponent attacks with two rapid punches, which you slap sideways as you step back out of range, and then step forward to follow up with chops to his neck.

BACKGROUND

The Book of Balance and Harmony is a collection of writings from a master of the Complete Reality School of Taoism in the 13th century CE. In the book there is a reference to 'stroke the lute to summon the phoenix', a metaphor for concentrating the mind to nourish the spirit when meditating. In the same way the many changes into 'Seven Stars'/'Stroke the Lute' in the Long Form represent focusing on a new opponent or fresh attack.

15 Deflect, Parry and Punch

DESCRIPTION

This technique can be done either stepping forward or stepping back. Step forward or back onto the left heel, extending the left hand and bringing the right fist back to the hip. Turn the body to the right, bringing the left palm across; this is Ban, 'to remove/deflect' (the same term occurs in *The Classic of Boxing*). Now turn to the left and bring the left arm down in a parry; finally punch straight ahead with the right fist, sliding the left hand towards the elbow joint.

This works the spine and legs.

TOP TIP
Use more body and less arm when deflecting and parrying.

MARTIAL APPLICATION

High: Side-step to the outside of the opponent's punch to the head, deflecting the punch with your palm and at the same time punching him in the ribs.

Low: Side-step to the outside of the opponent's punch to the body, parrying the punch and at the same time punching him in the ribs or kidney.

16 As if Shutting a Door

DESCRIPTION

The Chinese commonly use double swing doors. Slide the back of the left hand along the underside of the right arm, at the same time bringing the weight back and breathing in; the palms now face towards the body. Shift the weight forward, thrusting from the back leg and pushing with both hands. Breathe out on the push.

This move coordinates the breath with the actions of the legs and arms.

1

TOP TIP
The weight goes forward behind the push, not before it.

MARTIAL APPLICATION

A simplistic application of this move is against a double wrist-grab (ideally you should be alert enough to prevent the grab in the first place). Take a small step to the side, twisting the body and raising and crossing your arms in the same direction. This crosses the opponent's arms and breaks his grip, with the upward twisting pressure on his thumbs. Keeping his arms crossed, seize his wrists and crank his arms, ready to follow up with a strike.

17 Embrace Tiger, Return to Mountain

DESCRIPTION

After 'As if Shutting a Door' lower the hands, palms down, and, keeping the weight forward, turn the front foot in on the heel. Turn through 135 degrees on the heel of the back foot, turning the arms so that the palms face out. Shift the weight onto the right foot and raise the arms, straightening the back leg. This last move can be practised from side to side, to strengthen the joints and stimulate the circulation.

TOP TIP
Keep the arms and legs moving together.

MARTIAL APPLICATION

If the opponent grabs you around the waist and tries to throw you, get underneath him and lift, adding to his force. He is the tiger that you embrace and return to the mountain.

18 Cross Hands

DESCRIPTION

Step in with the back foot and cross the hands in front of the chest, keeping the knees bent. This position can be held with the eyes shut to strengthen the limbs.

BACKGROUND

The literal name for this technique is 'Figure Ten Hands' because two crossed sticks – one horizontal and one vertical – make the Chinese character for ten (though in Tai Chi the arms are diagonal).

TOP TIP

Don't raise the arms too high; you should be able to see between the crossed hands.

MARTIAL APPLICATION

When the opponent attacks with a roundhouse kick you step in, catching his leg in your crossed arms, then lift his leg and throw him to the ground.

19 Fist under Elbow

DESCRIPTION

From 'Cross Hands' turn the left foot out on the heel and reach over to the left with your left hand. Step out with the right foot into a front stance and reach over with the right arm. As you shift the weight onto the back foot, make fists (right fist under left elbow) and twist your body and limbs left. Twist right and shift the weight forward, opening the left fist as you turn the body to the left.

This technique twists and stretches the whole body.

TOP TIP
Make sure the left fist is pointing up at all times.

MARTIAL APPLICATION

The opponent attacks from the side with a punch to the head. You see this with your peripheral vision and step out, pulling his arm. He resists, so you change from pull to punch.

BACKGROUND

The Chinese term literally means 'Under Elbow See Fist'; the opponent sees your fist under his elbow.

20 Step Back and Repulse Monkey

DESCRIPTION

From the last position swing the arms round to the left, raising the front foot with the sole turned in. Then step back, giving a palm strike. The final position is the same as in 'Brush Knee Twist Step'.

This trains balance and coordination.

1

TOP TIP

The palm strike and the placing of the left foot on the ground should be simultaneous.

MARTIAL APPLICATION

You side-step and intercept the opponent's punch to the head, then strike him to the face to bend him back; continuing the palm pressure and using circular force, you trip him. The monkey has been repulsed.

BACKGROUND

The mischievous monkey being referred to is the hero of the 16th-century novel *Journey to the West*. In Chinese martial arts there is also a specific boxing method based on this character.

21 Needle at Sea Bottom

DESCRIPTION

Step forward, bringing the left hand up to protect the face, while the right hand comes up in an arc and then thrusts down; at the same time retract the left foot back onto the ball. The left foot steps forward into a front stance as the right arm comes up to shoulder level.

This technique stretches the spine.

1

TOP TIP
Keep the back straight,
even when inclining
forward.

MARTIAL APPLICATION

Side-step and intercept the opponent's
punch, striking him in the groin with the
ridge-bone above the thumb. Follow up
by grabbing his crotch and striking him
with the other hand.

BACKGROUND

The needle is the strike; the Sea of Qi is
the area of the body below the Dantian
(or Cinnabar Field, the point just below
the navel, considered to be the centre of
the body), so the groin or Sea Bottom is
the target.

22 Fan Through the Back

DESCRIPTION

'Fan Through the Back' is the most popular of a variety of names for this technique; the arm movement resembles a fan opening out. From 'Needle at Sea Bottom' turn the front foot in slightly, raising and crossing the arms. Step back slightly and open out the arms – the left arm extends forward in a palm strike, while the right arm is above the head; sink into a 'Horse-Riding Stance' at the same time.

This stimulates the circulation and the autonomic nervous system.

TOP TIP

In the final position, don't lock the left elbow joint; the right arm is extended above the head and the arm is rounded in shape.

1

MARTIAL APPLICATION

Evade, intercept and seize the opponent's
punching arm. Raise, twist and stretch
his arm, then strike it above the elbow.

23 Swing Fist

DESCRIPTION

From the last move, turn the front foot in on the heel and sit back, raising the right arm above the head and upper-cutting with the left fist. Turn the body, crossing the arms on the left side, fists clenched. Swing the arms in an arc, striking with the back of the right fist; the left palm is on top and the weight goes forward.

This technique manipulates the joints.

1

TOP TIP
This technique should be performed with a continuous wave-like motion.

MARTIAL APPLICATION

High: with peripheral vision you see the opponent's punch to the head, evade and parry it, countering with an upper-cut.

Low: facing you, the opponent attacks the body; you retreat and bounce his arm offline with your forearm. You seize his arm and back-fist him, followed by a palm strike.

24 Cloud Hands

DESCRIPTION

Turn to the left, drawing intersecting clockwise circles, while simultaneously shifting the weight and stepping to the left also.

This technique manipulates the joints and tendons, especially in the arms, and enhances the circulation.

TOP TIP
Here the arms are only slightly bent as they twist and turn.

①

MARTIAL APPLICATION

Side-step and intercept the opponent's punch and use his momentum to push him into a wall/pillar.

My former student, Alex Ferreras, used this technique to good effect in Chinese full contact against an opponent who kept charging him with straight kicks and punches: bull and matador.

BACKGROUND

This is sometimes translated as 'Wave Hands in Clouds', but the Chinese term means simply 'Cloud Hands', which is either a mistake or a pun. There is a similar-sounding Chinese character that means 'turning' and this is what the hands are doing; so the correct name is really 'Turning Hands'.

25 Pat the Horse High

DESCRIPTION

Turn left into a high 'Cat Stance', left foot forward; the left hand is low and the right hand is high, with the palms facing one another. Sink, bringing the hands in close together.

This technique stretches the lungs with the opening and closing of the rib cage.

TOP TIP
Don't splay the fingers.

Connections with *The Classic of Boxing*

The name of this technique appears in
The Classic of Boxing.

Gesture 3:
'Pat the horse, handed down from
Tai Zu.
The complete technique can be more
or less and can change.
In advancing, attacking, retreating and
dodging, weakness becomes strength.
If you receive a short punch from the
enemy, this method is best ...'

'Tai Zu' is a reference to the first
emperor of the Song dynasty (founded
960 CE). The message is to match the
technique to the opponent.

Later we have Gesture 8:
'... with heavy force change boxing
method.
Pat the Horse High while balanced.
Hit him once and cause his life to end.'

MARTIAL APPLICATION

Intercept the opponent's punch and palm-strike him in the face. The other hand comes behind his head, which you use as a lever to wrench his neck.

I have seen documentary footage of the Vietcong leader Ho Chi-Minh doing this technique on trainees. He was good.

Note how our circular force bends the opponent's head back and his back also, so that he is anything but 'centrally correct'.

26 Separate Hands

DESCRIPTION

Only in Wu style is there a name for this technique, although the posture does exist in other styles. The arms are extended, with the front hand palm upwards at head level, the back hand palm downwards and slightly lower as you step into a front stance. The angle between the arms is about 90 degrees and the focus is on the chopping reverse hand.

This technique can be held as a static posture to strengthen the arms.

TOP TIP

Get the focus correct; many people stare straight ahead, instead of focusing on the striking hand.

MARTIAL APPLICATION

Intercept the opponent's swing to the head while simultaneously chopping his neck. The defending hand is palm up, the striking hand palm down.

27 Tiger Embraces Head

DESCRIPTION

This technique can be practised in a 'Horse-Riding Stance', twisting the body and limbs from side to side. In the form you turn the front foot out slightly and, turning the body, clench the fists and cross the arms.

TOP TIP

Don't raise the crossed arms so high that your view is blocked.

MARTIAL APPLICATION

Side-step and intercept the opponent's punch to the head, slapping him in the back of the head with the other hand, and then pulling his head forward into a forearm smash.

Connections with *The Classic of Boxing*

Though not one of the 32 techniques of *The Classic of Boxing*, 'Tiger Embraces Head' is mentioned therein:

'... when tiger embraces head, there must be no door to hide'.

28 Drape the Body

DESCRIPTION

Keeping the arms crossed, open the hands, twisting them round in a clockwise direction, bending them in towards the body.

This manipulates the joints and tendons.

❶

TOP TIP
Make sure the arms and legs are in motion at all times.

2

MARTIAL APPLICATION

In a follow-up to 'Separate Hands',
bend the opponent's arm in and lock
it. Your body weight is draped over the
opponent's arm.

1

Note how as we put our body weight into the technique, we destroy the opponent's posture so that he is no longer 'centrally correct'.

29 Separate Feet

DESCRIPTION

As the arms are crossed, bring the back foot in towards the front foot in a half-circle and kick out with the ball of the foot at 45 degrees, extending the arms. The nose, front foot and arm should all point in the same direction. The rear arm extends back behind the head.

This move improves your balance.

TOP TIP
The rear arm should be higher than the front arm.

MARTIAL APPLICATION

Two opponents attack the head at the same time. Kick one and use 'Pat the Horse High' on the other.

30 Turn Body and Kick with Heel

DESCRIPTION

Retract the front leg and arm, and cross over the other leg and arm. Spin on the heel and ball of the foot through 45 degrees and kick out straight ahead as before, but this time kicking with the heel.

This is effective in training balance.

1

TOP TIP
The final arm position is the same as in 'Separate Feet'.

MARTIAL APPLICATION

The opponent suddenly grabs the shoulder from behind. Spin round in either direction, control his arms and stamp-kick him.

1

31 Step Forward Plant the Punch

DESCRIPTION

Put the foot down on the heel and draw a clockwise circle with the front arm. Shift the weight forward as you punch down through the circle with the other hand.

This is good for coordination.

TOP TIP
Keep the back straight as you incline forward.

MARTIAL APPLICATION

Catch the opponent's kick and flip him
onto the ground. Punch down.

32 Turn Body and Swing Fist

DESCRIPTION

Fold the arms and turn the front foot
in. Step across with the back foot into
a front stance, swinging the arms into a
back-fist and palm strike.

*This is beneficial for footwork
and balance.*

TOP TIP
This technique is like a
wave smashing down.

MARTIAL APPLICATION

The opponent attacks from the side.
You see him with your peripheral vision
and defend across the body with the
palm, following up with a back-fist and
palm strike.

33 Step Back Seven Stars

DESCRIPTION

Step back diagonally into a 'Seven Star'
arm position in a 'Back Stance'.
You can hold this position as a static
meditation with the eyes shut to train
your balance.

TOP TIP

Make sure that the front foot
and the fingers are pointing in
the same direction.

MARTIAL APPLICATION

Intercept the opponent's punch, stepping
back and pulling him down.

34 Beat the Tiger

DESCRIPTION

Step back into a 'Front Stance', with the right hand reaching over the left. Turn the rear foot out while pulling down, then turn around through 180 degrees into a 'Front Stance', with the front hand pushing up, the other hand pushing down; you can have open hands or fists.

This is good for stretching the whole body.

1

TOP TIP
Make sure that the back is straight as you incline forward.

2

3

MARTIAL APPLICATION

Side-stepping and intercepting the opponent's punch to the head, suddenly pull him forward and strike the back of his neck with a hammer fist.

BACKGROUND

'Beat the Tiger' is a reference to a story from the 14th-century novel called *The Water Margin*, which is about the adventures of 108 righteous bandits. One of them, Wu Song, after imbibing heavily, falls asleep on the mountainside and is awoken by a man-eating tiger that attacks him. He kills it with blows from his bare hands.

35 Drape Body and Kick

DESCRIPTION

Turning the front foot in and pivoting on the rear foot, swing the arms around in a big arc to the right side, sinking as you lower them. Raise the front foot and both arms, clenching the fists. Fists and foot should be in a line parallel to the centre line. Open and extend the arms at shoulder level; at the same time kick out at knee level.

This stretches and twists the whole body and is beneficial for the circulation.

TOP TIP

Do the turn, pivot and arm-swing in a continuous action.

MARTIAL APPLICATION

The attacker hits down on the head from the side. Turn and intercept his arm; pull and kick.

The leverage from the armlock bends the opponent's head forward and sets up the kick.

2

36 Box the Ears

DESCRIPTION

Lowering the foot and coming into a front stance, bring both arms down to either side in an arc, finishing in a double punch at head level.

This is good for the circulation and for flexing the shoulder joints.

TOP TIP

Get the weight going forward with the double punch.

2

MARTIAL APPLICATION

Retreat slightly, intercept and open out
the attacker's arms as he tries to grab
your neck; punch his ears or temples.
Follow up with a knee to the head.

37 **Parting the Wild Horse's Mane**

DESCRIPTION

Turning the front foot out, twist the body, with the front hand at face level, the other hand low to the side. Step forward into a front stance, opening the arms out at approximately a right-angle, front hand palm up, other hand palm down; the focus is on the front hand (note that this position is similar to 'Separate Hands', but the focus is different).

This opens and closes the ribcage and flexes the spine and the major joints in the limbs.

①

TOP TIP
Get the focus right and show that you mean business.

2

MARTIAL APPLICATION

Use 'Nine Palace Step' (see pages 68–71)
to evade the attacker's kick, slapping
it aside. The fingers of the other hand
thrust towards his face.

Note how the finger thrust to the face has broken the opponent's intent to attack.

2

38 Fair Lady Works Shuttle

DESCRIPTION

Turning the front foot out, twist the body, with the front hand at face level, the other hand low to the side. Step forward into a front stance, then come back onto the heel, swinging the front arm up and to the side; turn to the other side, bringing the arms into the chest. Turn back into a front stance, extending the arms palms out so that they face away from the head.

This form twists and stretches the limbs and spine.

TOP TIP
At the end of the technique the arms should frame the head.

1

MARTIAL APPLICATION

Sway out of range of the attacker's
swing and then move in, giving his own
force back to him.

1

②

BACKGROUND

The 'Fair Lady' (literally 'Jade Girl') in question is the diligent Weaver Girl of Chinese folklore, represented by the star Vega. After she got married she neglected her duties and so her father, the Sun God, only let her see her husband once a year, on the seventh night of the seventh month.

39 Snake Creeps Down (low style)

DESCRIPTION

Turn the back foot out and reach over with the left hand, with the other hand in at the chest; reach over with the right hand, then with the left hand again, turning the back foot out. Lower the hands, going into a back stance, then twist the body to bring the hands back, around and up in a big circle. Step into a front stance, with the hands in line, left hand high and right hand low.

This stimulates the autonomic nervous system and flexes the joints and spine.

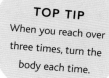

TOP TIP
When you reach over
three times, turn the
body each time.

③

④

⑤

⑥

MARTIAL APPLICATION

Side-step and intercept the opponent's
punch, pulling him forward; as he starts
to resist, change direction and give him
back his own force.

1

Note how lending our force to the opponent's resistance has totally destabilized him.

2

40 Golden Cockerel Stands on One Leg

DESCRIPTION

Carry on from 'Snake Creeps Down', lowering the left palm to groin level as you raise the right palm above the head; the right foot is raised, with the foot turned in. Both hands and the right foot are in a straight line that is parallel to the spine.

This technique trains your balance and gives the body a stretch; it can be done slowly and repeatedly on either side to improve blood circulation.

TOP TIP

Make sure that the hands and raised foot are parallel to the centre line.

As seen from the front

MARTIAL APPLICATION

In Tai Chi the upper hand can be a sliding defence and strike, or simply a direct strike; the lower hand is usually a defence, while the raised leg is either a kick or is used to block a low kick. There is no punch and no falling on top of the opponent. In Chen style this technique is also called 'Raise Lamp Towards Heaven'.

①

Connections with *The Classic of Boxing*

'Golden Cockerel Stands on One Leg' is one of the 32 illustrated postures in *The Classic of Boxing*.

Gesture 2:
'Golden Cockerel on One Leg, preparing to rise. Pull back the leg(s) while giving a crosswise punch.

Snatch with the Back, Reclining Ox double fall. After this my opponent incessantly complains to high heaven.'
The application mentioned in the poem is quite different from any Tai Chi application of 'Golden Cockerel Stands on One Leg' that I am aware of.

41 White Snake Spits out Tongue

DESCRIPTION

Lower the foot into a back stance, bringing the hands in front of the body, with left over right and palm up. Shift forward into a front stance, thrusting with the fingers of the left hand and kicking with the left foot.

This technique is useful for training your balance.

1

TOP TIP
Make sure that the kick and finger thrust are well extended, as you are in pursuit of a retreating opponent.

MARTIAL APPLICATION

Side-step and intercept the opponent's
punch to the head, giving a finger thrust
to his neck and grabbing his throat. As he
retreats, follow with a kick.

Note how the opponent's posture is destabilized as he first bends back then bends forward on receiving our counters.

42 Slap the Face

DESCRIPTION

Bring the hands around to the left side, stepping down into a front stance and slapping down with the left hand; the right hand protects the armpit.

This transition is a test of balance.

1

TOP TIP
The heel makes first contact with the ground and the weight then transfers onto the sole.

MARTIAL APPLICATION

Using 'Nine Palace Step', evade and
intercept the attacker's punch and palm-
strike him.

Be aware of the opponent's other hand.

We uncross the legs as we palm strike the opponent's face. Put the whole body weight into the technique.

43 Single Hand Sweep Lotus Leg

DESCRIPTION

Turn the front foot in and pivot on
the other foot, turning the body and
swinging the left arm around to the right
at shoulder level. Raise the right leg and
slap the foot with the left hand.

This gives a total body stretch.

TOP TIP

Make sure that foot and hand make contact, to complete the move.

2

MARTIAL APPLICATION

Using 'Nine Palace Step', evade and intercept the attacker's punch and chop him, at the same time sweeping the supporting leg.

2

BACKGROUND

In Wu-style 'Single Hand Sweep Lotus
Leg' and 'Double Hand Sweep Lotus Leg'
lifting the leg and bringing it across is said
to resemble a strong breeze sweeping
across an expanse of lotus flowers.

1

44 Punch the Groin

DESCRIPTION

Lower the foot and step forward, drawing a clockwise circle in front of the body with the left hand; at the same time the right fist draws a clockwise circle on the right side and ends in an upward punch through the first circle.

This form flexes the shoulder joints.

2

3

TOP TIP

Make sure that the weight goes behind the punch and not before it.

MARTIAL APPLICATION

Side-step and scoop up the opponent's kick, punching him in the groin.

45 Step back to ride the tiger

DESCRIPTION

Withdraw the front foot a little to come into a 'Cat Stance', then separate the arms and bring them up to the side, right hand palm open, left hand forming a hook. Pivot to the right, scooping down with the left hand and raising the right above the head and then kicking across.

The details of this technique in *The Classic of Boxing* seem to involve a lot of leg sweeps, which are not there in the Tai Chi version of the technique.

This trains balance and flexes the joints.

1

TOP TIP

Sink as the hands go down, rise as they come up.

MARTIAL APPLICATION

Evade and catch or scoop away the
first attacker's kick, while turning to
deflect the second attacker's punch
and countering with a kick.

Connections with *The Classic of Boxing*

This is another technique that appears in *The Classic of Boxing*.

Gesture 28:
'Ride Tiger Technique, move the body, Change legs and kick. I must move the legs without him realizing; Left and right sweep follows sweep.

His losing hands are easily separated by my cutting blades.'

The regular Tai Chi applications are quite different from those in *The Classic of Boxing*.

BACKGROUND

Zhang Daoling (34–156 CE) is sometimes called the first Taoist pope and there are many legends about him. He is sometimes depicted riding a tiger, showing his mastery over nature and emotion. Other Chinese worthies are occasionally also depicted thus, but Zhang is the best-known and most obvious candidate for the origin of the name of this technique.

46 **Double Hand Sweep Lotus Leg** (see also no. 43)

DESCRIPTION

Lower the foot, turn it in and pivot on the other foot as you turn, bringing the arms round to the right at shoulder level. Without turning the head, you can see the hands with your peripheral vision. Slap the foot with both hands, stepping back diagonally and pushing out with both hands.

This flexes the joints and tendons and trains your balance.

TOP TIP

Slap the foot with both hands or the technique is incomplete.

MARTIAL APPLICATION

Using 'Nine Palace Step', evade and smother the opponent's reverse punch and sweep his supporting leg.

47 Draw the Bow to Shoot the Tiger

DESCRIPTION

Turn the back foot out, lowering the
hands and swinging them round, back
and to the right as you turn the body.
Finish with a double punch.

This stretches the spine and the limbs.

BACKGROUND

The technique's name has the same derivation as the sword technique 'Li Guang Draws the Bow to Shoot the Tiger'. The body action and application are also very similar.

TOP TIP

Make sure that both fists are punching in the same direction.

MARTIAL APPLICATION

Again the tiger is a reference to the opponent. Side-step and brush aside the attacker's Shaolin-style double palm strike, countering with a double punch. In 1976 at the South-East Asian Chinese Pugilistic Championships in Singapore my Shaolin opponent tried to attack me in this way. I punched him in the face. Generally it is good to be direct.

Connections with *The Classic of Boxing*

The Classic of Boxing has a similar technique (except for the mention of kicks).

Gesture 10:
'Lie in Ambush Technique;
Bend the bow awaiting the tiger.
If he rushes into the trap,

He finds it difficult
to move away.
I then take the chance
to discharge continuous
kicks. When he receives the strikes, he
must be confused and afraid.'

48 Tai Chi in Unity

DESCRIPTION

Turn the front foot in slightly and thrust diagonally forward with the fingers of the right hand as the left hand comes back low. Step up with the back foot so that the feet are shoulder-width apart, bringing the hands into the chest, left over right. The knees should be bent.

Holding the arms in the extended position strengthens the joints and the circulation.

BACKGROUND

'Tai Chi in Unity' is followed by 'Completion Style', which is in fact Wu Chi (no. 1) again and thus represents a return to the beginning. However the journey you have undertaken has transformed you; in terms of internal alchemy, your Shen has been raised.

TOP TIP

The focus follows the finger thrust, then becomes neutral when the arms are crossed.

MARTIAL APPLICATION

Side-step and deflect the attacker's kick and finger-thrust to the face or neck.

Chapter 3

Proverbs KEY CONCEPTS OF TAI CHI

Going through the door

According to the *Song of the Thirteen Tactics*, 'To go through the door and be led along the path oral instruction is necessary.' In Chinese martial arts 'going through the door' refers to a student undergoing a ceremony of discipleship with his master, where he accepts the rules of the school. After this he is 'inside the door' and is referred to as a 'door person'. As such, he can start to learn aspects of the art that are not taught openly or written down in books, such as Neigong and the Six Secret Words.

This type of ritual initiation was once widespread, but was banned in China for many years as a feudalistic custom; according to martial artists in China to whom I'd talked, it has become common practice again. In 1999 I visited a full-time martial-arts school near the Purple Cloud Temple on Wudang Mountain. They told me that, on arrival, new recruits went through an initiation in front of statues of Tai Chi's legendary founder, Zhang Sanfeng, and of Zhen Wu (True Warrior), the main god of the mountain.

In my Sifu's school, students were normally given the chance to become disciples after three to twelve months of committed training. We agreed to accept the rules of the school and bowed in front of a portrait of Zhang Sanfeng, and then bowed to our Sifu. I was taught in this way and I follow the same tradition, which recognizes and rewards a student's dedication.

Another aspect of oral transmission are the five Tai Chi Chuan Classics (see opposite); all are in the form of ditties, so they are designed to be memorized and chanted. As a youth, my teacher was required by his Sifu to memorize and chant the Classics during Neigong training, but I know of no one who does this now.

My Sifu, Cheng Tin-hung, never attended a Tai Chi class in his life; as a teenager he was taught on a one-to-one basis, first by his uncle, Cheng Wing-kwong, and later by Master Qi Minxuan.

Sifu Cheng ran both morning and evening classes on his Hong Kong rooftop. Sometimes he would stay downstairs and watch TV or play mah-jong, and at other times he would come upstairs and walk around, smoking a cigarette. Sometimes he would actually talk to us (he spoke only Cantonese) or show us a technique. After some months I became closer to him and would often take meals or walks with him. During these encounters I learned a great deal from him about Chinese culture in general, and about Tai Chi theory and practice in particular. On one occasion we were discussing some martial concepts from the Classics in the presence of one of his senior Chinese female assistants. After a bit, obviously frustrated, she interjected to say that she didn't understand. Sifu said dismissively, 'You are not at his level.' This was oral transmission indeed.

The Tai Chi Chuan Classics

Tai Chi is a marriage of theory and practice. There are those who can recite the Tai Chi Chuan Classics, but aren't really very good at Tai Chi. There are others who are competent at Tai Chi, but whose ignorance of the theory prevents them from progressing further. There are some who know no theory and whose skill level is also low. It is said there are even some who have mastered both theory and practice.

Nobody really knows who wrote the five Tai Chi Chuan Classics, but they have been in existence in their present form since around 1852. They borrow extensively from the *Book of Changes*, Sunzi's *The Art of War* and the writings of Taoist philosophers, especially Laozi. They are not always easy to read or logical, as the texts seem to be full of interpolations; they overlap and are repetitious. Some Classics are more valuable than others; and the material in each Classic is not necessarily all at the same level. There is also much that is not to be found in the Classics.

However, the Classics are the main source of Tai Chi theory, and we will look to them for advice as we go along. My old Sifu would often give random quotes from the Classics as explanations, and in later years I studied them in depth with him.

Duality and change

Most of the key concepts that underpin the practice of Tai Chi can be found in the five texts known as the Tai Chi Chuan Classics; they are listed in the Appendix (see page 376). In this chapter these concepts are explored using appropriate quotations from the Classics, together with commentary based on many years of practice, teaching and exchange. The Classics are not a coherent body of work and there is some overlap of material.

The basic duality in Tai Chi comprises Yin and Yang. Yin and Yang each contain a dot of the other and this is what creates the capacity for change. The changes of Yin and Yang are the essence of Tai Chi.

'If there is up there is down, if there is forward there is back, if there is left there is right. If there is intent to go up, intent to go down is there immediately. If you raise something up, there is intent to smash it down with increased force, thus severing its roots.'
The Tai Chi Chuan Discourse

In Tai Chi theory when we do something to an extreme, it reverts to its opposite. This is true from a health perspective as well as from a martial perspective. For example, many form movements are wave-like and go from low to high or high to low. Likewise we can 'go up' by raising the opponent's attacking arm, as in 'Fist under Elbow', thus opening his rib cage and making it more vulnerable when we 'go down' and hit it. In throwing techniques like 'White Crane Flaps its Wings' we raise the opponent's body, thus severing his root in order to smash it.

'Each place has its individual balance of void and substantial.'
The Tai Chi Chuan Discourse

Fist under elbow

Four Directions

Most of the time, when doing Tai Chi forms, pushing hands and applications, one foot is full of weight while the other is empty. The weight goes with the technique. If we pull, the weight comes back; if we push, the weight goes forward and the rear foot is empty. When the weight is evenly distributed, both feet are full; the upper body is empty and has the potential for change.

One of the key aims of pushing hands drills such as 'Four Directions' is to create a muscle memories that the foot and weight changes to and from void and substantial become second nature.

'Once there is movement there is separation; once there is stillness there is unity. Nothing is exaggerated, nothing is lacking.'
The Canon of Tai Chi Chuan

Movement produces the separation of Tai Chi into Yin and Yang, as at the beginning of the hand form or in self-defence. Stillness and the unity of Yin and Yang in Tai Chi occur at the end of the hand form or after self-defence. All is done to the appropriate degree – neither more, nor less.

'Suddenly conceal, suddenly reveal. When the left feels heavy, then make it empty. When the right feels heavy, then make it distant. When the opponent looks up, I am still higher, when he looks down I am lower still.'
The Canon of Tai Chi Chuan

In *The Art of War* the strategist Sunzi wrote, 'Warfare is the Way of deception.' And it is just so when applying Tai Chi; we change in accordance with the opponent's actions and reactions. We absorb his attacks by confronting him with emptiness. This is done by dodging and side-stepping. When the opponent's attack is going up, we raise it even higher; when it is going down, we take it even lower.

So in applying 'Step Back and Repulse Monkey' we can pull and press the opponent forward when he attempts to punch and when he resists we simply reverse the direction of our force.

'Always remember, once there is movement, there is nothing that does not move. Once there is stillness, there is nothing that is not still.'

Interpretation of the Practice of the Thirteen Tactics

Whether we are doing forms, pushing hands or applications, we should use total body force and not just the arms and legs. Equally, when we are still, we should not fidget or move unnecessarily.

'There is stillness even where there is movement. When there is movement there is stillness.'

Song of the Thirteen Tactics

Whether doing forms, pushing hands or applications, the face remains composed (apart from the eyes, which change their gaze according to the technique). Normally there is no independent head movement (this trains peripheral vision). The mind remains unperturbed. Even when we are still, the circulation and breath are moving.

Repulse Monkey

Break Open Door

Force and forces

'By practice and familiarity, we gradually come to understand force. By understanding force, we can achieve enlightenment. However, we must be diligent over a long period of time and can't suddenly become expert.'
The Canon of Tai Chi Chuan

Whether it is hard or soft, the general Chinese term for the type of force that we use in Tai Chi is 'Jin'. As it represents a combination of strength and technique, 'Jin' can be considered to be educated force. So in applying 'Break Open the Door', the whole body weight is behind our hammer first when we strike the opponent.

The Fighter's Song mentions, but doesn't really explain, the Eight Forces:
'Peng, Lu, Ji, An must be taken seriously. Up and down accompany one another and the opponent finds it difficult to enter. Let him attack with great force; use four grams to displace 1,000 kilos.
'Cai, Lie, Zhou and Kao are even more amazing; when using them there is no need to think about it.'

Peng is upward force, Lu is sideways diversion, Ji is push and An is press; Cai is uproot, Lie is spiral, Zhou is forearm and Kao is barging with the shoulder/body. The forces can be used singly or in a wide variety of combinations.

'Entice the opponent into the void/emptiness. Harmonize and promptly discharge.'
The Fighter's Song

Eight Forces

PENG

LU

JI

AN

CAI

LIE

ZHOU

KAO

Break Arm Style

This means that we dodge and/or sidestep and/or redirect the opponent's attack so that there is nothing for him to hit — just a void. As I tell my Spanish students, 'He is the bull, we are the matador.' Generally Tai Chi parries are designed to dissipate/divert/absorb an opponent's attacks, thus unbalancing him rather than opposing him. However, sometimes (especially against weapon attacks) sudden sharp defence is used to bump his attacks offline and into emptiness. We promptly discharge by counter-attacking whenever and wherever there is an opening.

'If you can be light and agile, you can understand force. Achieve it inside a circle, not with hands and feet disorganized.'
The Fighter's Song

It takes less effort to be light and agile; it is also quicker to move if you are agile than if you are stiff and tense. Many Tai Chi techniques, whether defensive or offensive, are round or circular and therefore smooth. They can thus be quicker than linear techniques, which need to stop and start. So in 'Break Arm Style' for example there is considerable spinal rotation. Hands and feet should be strategically positioned to deal with attacks; this generally means that they need to point towards the attacker.

The Three Treasures

The Three Treasures of Chinese internal alchemy are Qi or vital force/energy (including the breath and circulation), Jing or vital essence (saliva, sweat, semen and other body secretions) and Shen or spiritual energy. According to Chinese internal alchemy, the more of each of the Three Treasures we have, the healthier we become and the greater our prospects for longevity. Likewise, when there is a lack of (or problem with) one of the Three Treasures, there is an adverse effect on the other two.

'Let the Qi sink to the Dantian.'
The Canon of Tai Chi Chuan

This is what is meant by abdominal breathing. The Dantian (literally 'Cinnabar Field') being referred to above is a point just below the navel. As far as Qi is concerned, through Tai Chi practice the body becomes more relaxed. The diaphragm is able to sink, making it possible for the lungs to take in more air and expand downwards. The increased supply of Qi/air stimulates the production of haemoglobin and the removal of waste products from the body. It is not a mysterious process.

Abdominal breathing is further enhanced by a great variety of contracting and expanding exercises in Neigong, hand- and weapon-form training and pushing hands drills. This type of contracting and expanding also makes self-defence techniques more effective.

'The abdomen is spongy. The Qi is hoarded to enter the bones. The spirit is at ease and the body is tranquil; this must be deeply engraved on the mind.'
Interpretation of the Practice of the Thirteen Tactics

A spongy, relaxed abdomen is vital for developing abdominal breathing. A spongy abdomen also helps to absorb the force and shock of an opponent's blows. The physical activity of Tai Chi manipulates the joints and aids in the production of synovial fluid, which helps the bone marrow to continue supplying blood cells. This is one of two references in the *Interpretation of the Practice of the Thirteen Tactics* to Qi entering the bones; and strong bones are a prerequisite for physical activity.

There are formal ritualistic postures at the beginning of the hand form to prepare the body and mind for the journey that is the form. Thus the spirit is at ease and the body is tranquil.

'In the attainment of perfection do not waste Kung Fu (effort). Carve and carve again into the mind that it should be on the waist. Internally the abdomen is relaxed and still and the Qi ascends.'
Song of the Thirteen Tactics

We should concentrate on what is important and not get sidetracked. We know the centre line is the key to body movement.

The abdomen should be relaxed and should not move excessively when the diaphragm is expanding and contracting in harmony with the lungs. I once saw a huge American Tai Chi instructor demonstrate his 'Qi pump': he made tiny little hand and leg movements while massively contracting and expanding his enormous gut. It was very funny to watch. Good Tai Chi it was not.

Whatever we are doing in Tai Chi, the basic breathing method is the same. We breathe in and out through the nose. The mucous membrane in the nose filters the air and warms it before it enters the lungs, thus helping to prevent throat and chest infections. While breathing this way, the tongue is pressed against the roof of the mouth as an aid to salivation. Saliva is a body secretion and therefore a type of Jing. A dry mouth is uncomfortable and unhealthy, thus affecting the Shen. So from both a Western and a Chinese perspective, the Three Treasures are very much interrelated.

'The Qi should be excited to activity while the Shen should be internally hoarded.'
The Tai Chi Chuan Discourse

Tai Chi training, of whatever kind, should stimulate the breath and circulation while we remain calm.

'Use the mind to move the Qi; try to let it sink in an orderly manner, then it can accumulate and enter the bones. Use the Qi to move the body. Try to let it move without hindrance, then we can conveniently act according to the mind.'
Interpretation of the Practice of the Thirteen Tactics

We use the mind to concentrate on fundamentals like balance, posture, coordination and smoothness of movement. This will lead to correct breathing and improved circulation. We don't actually try to use the mind to send Qi to different parts of the body, as our Tai Chi training is doing this already. Studies have shown that regular exercise such as Tai Chi helps to preserve and even increase bone-mass density, so it seems that the Qi does enter our bones.

'Move the Qi as through a pearl with nine crooked paths. It goes smoothly everywhere.'
Interpretation of the Practice of the Thirteen Tactics

The first Dantian (Cinnabar Field) is located between the eyes; the second is at heart level, while the third is just below the navel. All are centrally aligned. Each of the three Dantians is said to have nine cavities. *The Yellow Emperor's Classic of Internal Medicine* (traditional dated to 2696–2598 BCE) talks about the nine orifices. The head, neck, shoulders, elbows, wrists, waist, hips, knees and ankles are the nine major body sections. The nine paths could be any of these, and become crooked when we move. This is a poetic way of saying that, through the contracting and expanding movements of Tai Chi, the Qi goes everywhere.

'From the ability to inhale and exhale properly comes the ability to be nimble and flexible. By constantly developing the Qi there is no evil.'
Interpretation of the Practice of the Thirteen Tactics

By learning to breathe in and out through the nose, and by developing abdominal breathing, we feel comfortable whatever we are doing.

'In moving back and forth, the Qi sticks to the back. It amasses and enters the spine. Internally it strengthens the Jingshen (vigour), externally one exhibits peaceful ease.'
Interpretation of the Practice of the Thirteen Tactics

This is a direct reference to Taoist internal alchemy and to complex theories on orbits of circulation of the Three Treasures. It is not a necessary part of Tai Chi and can lead to mental and physical problems if practised incorrectly. Just as Qi (in the sense of breath and circulation) is stimulated by Tai Chi training, so are Jing and Shen. If there are problems with Jing, there will be problems with Shen and vice versa, and there will be a lack of vigour. The autonomic nervous system and the production of body secretions are stimulated by the sinking, rising and stretching involved in stance work. The operation of the central nervous system is enhanced by postural stretching and realignment.

'Body and intent are entirely concentrated on the vigour, not on the Qi; if on the Qi there is stagnation. If there is Qi there is no strength; if there is no Qi then there is great strength. The Qi is like the wheel of a chariot, the waist is like the axle.'

Interpretation of the Practice of the Thirteen Tactics

Here the focus is on Qi in the sense of the breath. No matter what we are doing in Tai Chi, we should concentrate on *that* activity and not on the breath. If the breath is audible and we are out of breath, then there is no stamina and no strength. If the breath is inaudible after exertion, then there is plenty of endurance and strength. Breath and centre-line movement drive the body and depend on one another like a wheel and an axle.

'The Qi circulates throughout the body without the slightest obstacle.'

Song of the Thirteen Tactics

Good Tai Chi technique leads to good circulation and vice versa.

'Freely contract and extend. Open and close and listen. Kung Fu (effort) is unceasing. Cultivate the method yourself. Let us enquire into what acts as the rule for the body in all this. The intent and Qi are the rulers; the bones and flesh are the officials.'

Song of the Thirteen Tactics

The arms, legs and body contract and extend in accord with the techniques. Defensive moves usually involve contracting; attacks such as kicks and punches involve extending. When we raise the arms we open the rib cage; when we lower the arms we close it – this stretches the lungs and adds power to the technique. While doing all this we need to listen to/feel what the opponent is doing. We learn by doing. By focusing on our aims and correct breathing, the body does what we want.

'Think and enquire where does the final purpose lie? It lies in seeking longevity and keeping a youthful appearance.'
Song of the Thirteen Tactics

One of the aims of Taoism is 'Long life, not old'. By this the Chinese mean longevity without the infirmities of old age. This is also the aim of Tai Chi. Lifestyle plays a part, too; smoking 100 cigarettes a day, as my old Sifu did, is inadvisable.

'If you don't enquire into the subject in this way you vainly waste time and Kung Fu (energy) and heave a sigh.'
Song of the Thirteen Tactics

This is the third reference to Kung Fu in the Song of the Thirteen Tactics. Here again it means time and energy. Tai Chi without Kung Fu is empty.

Focus

Focus refers to the correct alignment of the parts of the body that are involved in each technique.

'When attacking you should sink and be completely relaxed, concentrating on one direction.'
Song of the Thirteen Tactics

When performing a straight front kick, for example, the foot, fingers and nose should all be centred on one direction: the opponent. Sinking and relaxing at the same time helps to generate thrust from the legs and get the body weight behind the technique. This is what is meant by 'focus', and correct focus is essential for the effective application of all techniques.

The writings of General Qi Jiguang (1528–87) and Chang Naizhou (1724–83?) both talk about the 'three-tip' rule for spears: when on guard or thrusting, the spear tip, the nose tip and the front-foot tip should normally be pointing in the same direction. Centuries later the principles are the same. A lack of focus when executing forms is a sure sign that a Tai Chi practitioner does not know what he or she is doing.

Separate feet

Intent

The practitioner's Yi (intent) is expressed in the eyes and helps to give meaning to the technique.

'Make the source of fulfilling the intent at the waist. During the changes and turnings of void and substantial, always maintain the intent. The Qi circulates throughout the body without the slightest obstacle.'
Song of the Thirteen Tactics

When practising or dealing with an opponent, be ready to turn the body and/or flex the body forward or back. No matter whether evading, hitting or stepping, keep focused on what you want to do. Don't tense up and the breath and circulation will be fine.

'The intent and the Qi must be able to interact nimbly so there is a delightful roundness and liveliness. This is what is meant by the changes of void and substantial.'
Interpretation of the Practice of the Thirteen Tactics

Where the intent goes, the technique goes. The intent needs to be focused and calm for the technique to be smooth and efficient. The breath and circulation can then harmonize with the intent and the technique. Breathing is controlled, so the lungs are never completely filled or emptied of air; this is what is meant by the 'changes of void and substantial'. So if your Running Thunder Hand is blocked you follow up with another strike immediately.

'In accordance with the opponent, my movements appear mysterious. Every tactic lives in the mind. The principle is to use the intent.'
Song of the Thirteen Tactics

Running Thunder Hand

Do what the opponent doesn't expect. Apply techniques with intelligence and discrimination. Be clear about what you want to do and how to do it.

'The force is broken, but the intent is unbroken.'
The Fighter's Song

This particularly important piece of advice can be understood in two ways. When an opponent finishes his attack – whether successful or not – his technique can be said to be broken, but his intent to continue to try and do you harm is unbroken, so beware. Likewise, when you finish your attack on an opponent – whether successful or not – your technique can be said to be broken, but your intent to continue to try and do him harm is unbroken. The aim is to destroy, or distract, the opponent's intent while maintaining your own intent.

Double-weightedness

'With double-weightedness there is a hindrance; you can often see people who have practised their skills for several years who cannot change and turn. This leads them to being entirely ruled by others. They are not even aware they have this sickness of double-weightedness. If we wish to be free from this sickness, we must know Yin and Yang. When adherence is simply moving and when moving is simply adherence; when Yin does not depart from Yang, when Yang does not depart from Yin; when Yin and Yang serve one another, then we can say we understand force. After we understand force, the more we train, the more expert we become.'

The Canon of Tai Chi Chuan

Many Tai Chi instructors completely misunderstand the highly important concept of double-weightedness, believing it to be when there is an equal amount of weight put on each foot – something they themselves do every time they begin and end their Tai Chi forms. Some even talk of single-weightedness, which is nonsense.

Years ago at an Edinburgh seminar an American former pro-football player told me in front of everyone that the arm-bar technique 'Drape the Body' did not work. He attacked and I tried to put on the arm-bar. He resisted immediately (he was bigger and much stronger than me). For me to have tried to force the technique would have been double-weightedness. I didn't. Instead I softened and relaxed my arms; he relaxed a bit, too. Suddenly and sharply I slammed the technique on. His arm was not okay for a long time afterwards, but at least he knew the technique worked.

Double-weightedness

Total body force

'The whole body should be light and agile and linked together ... The root is in the feet, the legs discharge, the waist controls. The appearance is in the hands and fingers. From the feet to the legs all must be completely uniform and together, whether going forward or back. This will result in good timing and correct movement. This is controlled by the intent. Every part of the body is strung together without the least break.'

The Tai Chi Chuan Discourse

Tai Chi beginners tend to move their hands and arms, and lack the foot and body movement that gives power to techniques. Their centre of gravity is often too high, so there is no thrust from the legs when doing expansive movements. The waist provides rotation and flexion of the spine, which helps to give techniques focus. When the intent is there, the technique is there.

'No place is deficient or defective; no place has hollows or bumps; no place is cut off or over-extended.'

The Tai Chi Chuan Discourse

Nothing should be lacking. The backside, elbows and knees should not stick out and the neck should not be bent. There should be a full extension of the arms and legs, but without locking the joints or overbalancing. Bad technique is less effective and causes speed, mobility and balance problems.

BUMPS & HOLLOWS

CUT OFF

OVER EXTENDED

'Transport the Jin (force) like a hundred-times-refined steel. What firmness can it not break? The appearance is like a hawk seizing a hare. The spirit is like a cat catching a rat.'

Interpretation of the Practice of the Thirteen Tactics

Through repeated practice our use of force becomes highly efficient, with no unnecessary movements. We are the predator and the opponent is our prey. We attack them when they are in motion. There is no escape for them.

'Accumulate the force as if drawing a bow. Discharge the Fa Jin (force) as if releasing an arrow. Seek the straight amidst the bent. Accumulate, then discharge.'

Interpretation of the Practice of the Thirteen Tactics

In the Tai Chi Long Form we have the technique 'Draw the Bow to Shoot the Tiger'. We sweep the opponent's attack aside and fire a double punch at his head and ribs. The arms and legs bend to defend; they extend to hit. However, following the principle of Yin in the Yang and Yang in the Yin, we don't lock the joints. Locking the joints damages them and causes us to stiffen up; we need to unlock them before we can move again.

'The strength comes from the spine.'

Interpretation of the Practice of the Thirteen Tactics

This is centre-line theory, a theory not restricted to Tai Chi. The spine is the exact centre of the body. When we do forward-directed pushes and punches, the spinal column – and therefore the body weight – needs to be behind the technique. Force = Mass x Acceleration. Likewise, when we do a turning or swinging technique such as a pull, we need to rotate the body along the spinal axis.

'To receive is to release. If contact is broken, then resume the connection.'
Interpretation of the Practice of the Thirteen Tactics

As soon as we receive the opponent's attack, we release our counter to it. If we lose contact with the opponent, we immediately regain contact with him, so that we can feel and control what he is doing.

'By using the curve to gather the force there is more than sufficiency.'
Interpretation of the Practice of the Thirteen Tactics

When kicking or punching the opponent we don't lock our joints; this prevents damage on impact and makes transition into another technique quicker. It also means that the arms and legs are never fully straightened, but always slightly curved on extension. The same applies when doing techniques in forms. This is represented by the dot of Yin in the Yang in the Tai Chi symbol.

'The mind acts as the commander. The Qi acts as the flag. The waist is the banner.'
Interpretation of the Practice of the Thirteen Tactics

The body is like an army, working as a unit, but controlled by the mind, the Qi and the centre line.

'First seek to expand, then seek to be compact. Then you can achieve fine work neatly done. First in the mind, then in the body.'
Interpretation of the Practice of the Thirteen Tactics

Beginner's movements tend to be large and expansive. Gradually, through practice, they become more refined and efficient. First you need to think about what you are doing and then, when you have built muscle memory, it becomes second nature.

Retreat in Order to Advance

①

Footwork

'Step Forward, Move Back, Face Left, Look Right and Centrally Stable are Metal, Wood, Water, Fire and Earth.'
The Tai Chi Chuan Discourse

Earth is the key element, because all the others are found in or on it. In Tai Chi terms, when we begin and end centrally stable in a fight or other sudden situation, in between we need to move the feet if we can.

This footwork is trained to some extent in the hand form, though it contains little side-stepping. Footwork is trained much more in the weapon forms; and it is trained most of all in pushing hand drills such as 'Seven Star Step' and 'Nine Palace Step', and in related hand and weapon applications.

'The steps come from the changes of the body.'
Interpretation of the Practice of the Thirteen Tactics

The key is to use appropriate footwork for the technique that the body is attempting to apply.

Timing

'Furthermore, the trick is that if the opponent doesn't move, then I don't move; if the opponent starts to move, then I move first. Seem relaxed, but don't relax. Be prepared to move, but don't move.'
The Fighter's Song

The matching of our timing to the movements of our opponent is trained in moving-step pushing hands drills such as 'Seven Star Step' (normally the first thing I teach students). Skill in timing also results from training in a wide range of Tai Chi applications with a variety of partners.

Tai Chi is largely a counter-attacking style. There are three timings. 'After' is when we respond to an attack too late or not at all. 'During' is when we only just manage to parry/counter the attack. 'Before' is when we detect and pre-empt the attack; this is the ideal, and this is what *The Fighter's Song* is talking about.

To seem relaxed, but not to relax, seems paradoxical, but it means to be relaxed and alert, not droopy or flaccid – and to be prepared to move in any direction.

'If the opponent's actions are swift, then my response is swift; if his actions are slow, then I follow them slowly.'
The Canon of Tai Chi Chuan

Again the advice is to match the speed of our movements to the speed of our opponent's movements.

Pre-emptive Running Thunder Hand

'A feather cannot be added, a fly cannot land. Nobody knows me; I alone know them.'

The Canon of Tai Chi Chuan

This well-used idea is a rather poetic way of saying that in a fight we aim to be totally aware of our opponent's actions, while he has no idea of our intentions.

'Other schools of martial arts are numerous, but although there are external differences, they only amount to the strong bullying the weak; the slow surrendering to the fast. It is entirely due to innate ability and not at all related to having learned the skilful use of strength. From the sentence, "Use four

grams to displace 1,000 kilos" it's clear we don't use force to gain the upper hand. If you see an old man of eighty withstand the assault of a group of people, how can it be due to speed?'
The Canon of Tai Chi Chuan

The message of this comment is that in Tai Chi we don't normally oppose force with force. The admonition to use four grams ($^1/_{10}$ oz) to displace 1,000 kg (2,200 lb) is also to be found in *The Fighter's Song*; it means that we evade/absorb/dissipate the opponent's attacks rather than oppose them.

'Stand like a level scale, move like a wheel. Sink the weight on one side, then follow.'
The Canon of Tai Chi Chuan

Our shoulders are level and the spine is straight. We turn the body by rotating the spine as we receive our opponent's attack. At the same time we shift the weight forward or back, as appropriate.

'Silently memorize, study and imitate. Gradually we reach the point where we can do all we wish. Originally it is giving up yourself to follow the opponent. Many err by forsaking what is near to pursue what is far. A minute discrepancy leads to an error of 100 miles. The student must carefully discriminate.'
The Canon of Tai Chi Chuan

It is not enough to train unthinkingly. We should always be refining our technique and seeking to be more accurate and capable of a trained response. We don't move in a disordered way, but in accord with our opponent. Counter-attack to the nearest targets. Small errors lead to big errors.

Distance

'When the opponent advances, the distance seems surpassingly long; when he retreats, the distance seems surpassingly short.'
The Canon of Tai Chi Chuan

If we and our opponent start off at a fighting distance, we are both slightly out of range and need to step in to hit or grab one another. In Tai Chi, when an opponent steps in and invades our space with an attack, we can bend or step back to bring our target area out of range; then suddenly we follow up and close the distance with our counter-attack before he can recover. This is the Chinese military strategy of retreating in order to advance.

Suspended head-top

Many Tai Chi practitioners misunderstand this concept and take it to mean that the head-top appears as if suspended from the ceiling of the room in which they are practising. This is wrong. A perusal of the Internet will reveal that masters of the past and present all incline forward in their forms to some degree, although their backs are straight.

'Empty the neck and head-top of strength and the Qi sinks to the Dantian. Don't lean to either side or forward or back.'
The Canon of Tai Chi Chuan

By avoiding stiffness in the neck and maintaining correct posture – a straight line from the crown of the head to the tailbone – we develop abdominal breathing. There are three Dantian/Cinnabar Fields, and the one referred to here is the exact centre of the body just below the navel. The Qi (breath) does not actually go to the Dantian, but the effect of inhalation and exhalation can be seen and felt there.

The warning to avoid leaning refers to form and Neigong practice, where we keep a straight back, though it can be inclined forward. Leaning in all directions is a normal part of pushing hands and self-defence.

'If the Jingshen (vigour) can be raised, then there is no need to worry about leaning the weight to one side; this is what is meant by suspended head-top.'
Interpretation of the Practice of the Thirteen Tactics

In internal alchemy, spinal alignment is crucial for the Jing to travel up the spine and become Shen. From a Western perspective, the central nervous system runs through the spinal column; bad spinal posture will adversely affect the functioning of the central nervous system. So keep the spine aligned and straight.

'When standing, the body should be Zhong Zheng (centrally correct) and at ease, ready to deal with attacks from the Eight Directions.'
Interpretation of the Practice of the Thirteen Tactics

In self-defence don't stiffen, maintain good posture in the form of spinal alignment, and destroy and upset the opponent's posture, then regain good posture yourself.

'When the coccyx is Zhong Zheng (centrally correct), the spirit connects with the head-top. The whole body feels light and agile when the head-top is suspended. Be meticulous and keep the mind on enquiring into the art.'
Song of the Thirteen Tactics

The term Zhong Zheng (centrally correct) comes from Chinese meditation; it can be found in the *Nei Ye* (*Internal Work*) of c. 500 BCE. When doing Tai Chi there should be a straight line from the coccyx to the head-top, though this line is not always erect. It aligns the spine, neck and cerebral cortex; it is easier to move in a coordinated way when you have good posture as described here. Think about what you are doing when you practise.

Reeling silk

'Move the way a cat walks. Mobilize the force as if reeling silk from a cocoon.'
Interpretation of the Practice of the Thirteen Tactics

Cats move in a poised and balanced way. If you reel silk from a cocoon jerkily, it will break; the ideal is to be smooth. In the Wu Tai Chi lineage, of which I am part, there is a specific 'Reeling Silk' pushing hands drill, which trains the advanced skill of 'Gyrating Arms'. The idea is to develop the skill of returning to the opponent the force of his own strike or block. Chen Tai Chi stylists do not subscribe to this classic and mean something quite different by reeling silk.

'**Moving back and forth there must be turning over and folding up. In advancing and retreating there must be turning and change. Ultimate softness then becomes the hardest and firmest.**'

Interpretation of the Practice of the Thirteen Tactics

While applying these skills we often turn over and fold up our arms, and sometimes the arms of the opponent too. Going back and forward (note again the emphasis on footwork), we need to turn the body and change from Yin to Yang or Yang to Yin, as appropriate. The more relaxed we are, the more power we can generate.

Gyrating arms

Turning over and folding up

The uprooting wave

'Be still as a lofty mountain, move like a mighty river.'
The Interpretation of the Thirteen Tactics

Tai Chi trains us to be balanced/centrally stable and to root our feet to the ground, so that we are as stable as a mountain when at rest. When moving, the use of total body force is like a mighty river, sweeping all before it.

'This Chang Chuan (Long Boxing), it's like the great river, the Changjiang, surging and flowing without interruption.'
The Tai Chi Chuan Discourse

My Tai Chi spear form contains the technique 'The Waves Rising and Falling'. The hand form, and more specifically the sword form, that I teach contain many wave-like movements, with the body rising and sinking in accordance with the technique. All these water references are connected to the Tai Chi concept of Cai Lang – the uprooting wave.

Some years ago, at the Tai Chi Caledonia event in Scotland, I was translating for the Chen-style teacher and All-China Taijiquan Champion Wang Haijun, at a forum discussing pushing hands. However, I deliberately did not translate all that he said. He referred to a concept called Lan Cai Hua and I knew that the only other person present who knew what he was talking about was the only other Chinese Sifu present. Trying to translate and explain what was meant was not appropriate, given the time constraints and the level of the participants. It is also another of Tai Chi's poisoned chalices.

To the best of my knowledge very little has been written about this subject in either Chinese or English, even by such prolific scribes as Dr Yang Jwing-ming and Mr Robert W. Smith. It is time to remedy that.

Let us first examine some Chinese sources. My *Chinese Martial Arts Big Dictionary* mentions Lan / Luan Cai Hua, which is translated as 'Randomly Trampling/Stamping on Flowers'.

The dictionary goes on to state that the method is done using lively stepping and is not limited to one direction, nor is the number of steps restricted. There is no fixed training method; both partners are mutually intertwined in contact, so each can sense the other's changes in movement and technique. Each responds with Cai (here the character for uprooting) and trickery. They either divert/neutralize or discharge; stick, connect, adhere, follow, but don't break contact or resist. The footwork follows the advancing and retreating of the opponent and changes of position. Cai Lan Hua is Tuishou's highest level of training. This method helps to improve Ting (listening), Hua (diverting/neutralizing) and the ability to Fa (discharge).

All a bit nebulous, you might think. You are not wrong. However, many experienced Tai Chi practitioners don't have the skills listed.

Comrade Ma You-ching, a longterm disciple of the venerable Tai Chi historian Wu Tu-nan, edited a manual of Chinese martial-arts terms with the English title *Terms of Kung Fu* (although none of it is in English), which also deals with the subject of Lan Cai Hua. His Lan/Luan Cai Hua uses a different character for Cai than that found in the Wushu dictionary; it is the character that we use in Tai Chi to mean uproot.

Ma writes that Tuishou (pushing hands) has, in its shapes and appearances, certain kinds of level, such as the Jin (force) of holding and pointing (Qinna/seizing and holding and Dian Xue/attacking vital points), or nimble movement like a bee or a butterfly on a flower to gather or Cai its essence (Cai, which was used for uprooting earlier, now means 'gathering'). Ma says the name Cai Lan Hua was given by later generations.

Again, all a bit nebulous, you might think. You are not wrong. Again, many experienced Tai Chi practitioners don't have the skills listed.

Ma does, however, mention Cai Lang Hua (literally 'Uprooting/Gathering Wave Transforms') as being another name for Lan Cai Hua. This he does not explain. This

The Waves Rising and Falling

is, however, the precise name of an advanced pushing hands and fighting concept trained in the Wu lineage, but almost lost to the present generation.

Cai Lang Hua therefore is an advanced concept of uprooting with wave-like movement, which can be trained in pushing hands – mainly in moving step. The concept can be used in spear, sword, Die Pu (hitting) and making the opponent fall, Shuai Jiao (wrestling), Qinna (seizing and holding), and striking applications. The essence of the concept is: 'Use the Tao [Way] of the opponent and return it to the opponent's body.' The need for footwork is paramount as we ebb and surge in harmony with the actions of the opponent.

Cai Lang is not a secret concept, but it is also not something for beginners. I don't apologize for not translating Lan Cai Hua and trying to explain all this at Tai Chi Caledonia years ago. If I had, the participants would not have been waving, but drowning.

Chapter 4

Errant Knights

Arms and the armed – the Chinese tradition

Most Tai Chi books either ignore the subject of weapons altogether or mention it only in passing. I want to explore this rich and interesting topic by looking at the role of weapons in the Chinese cultural context, as well as at who used them and how.

In the Chinese tradition, as in Europe and Japan, people travelled mainly on foot or horseback and for self-protection would either have an armed escort or would carry arms themselves. Before the advent of firearms, these often included some type of traditional weapon such as a sabre, spear or double-edged sword. In Chinese martial arts there are three main types of weapon. Dao is any single-edged bladed weapon, ranging from a meat cleaver to a broadsword/sabre to a long, halberd-type weapon such as the Guan Dao. Qiang is a spear, normally at least 2 m (6 ft) long, with a pointed metal head. Jian is a double-edged sword, which can vary in length.

Most Tai Chi styles have some type of Dao form; some even having a double Dao method, or a Guan Dao form. All Tai Chi styles have some type of Jian form, some even having a double Jian method, while in Hao style they have also a short-sword method. However, while in many schools the forms are practised assiduously, the practical application either does not exist or is often sadly deficient.

The Dao was the weapon of the common soldier and the bandit, being versatile and effective at both medium and short range, while the Jian (with a slightly longer range and being a much more sophisticated weapon) was traditionally the badge of office of the scholar and military officer. For example, my ex-wife's Hong Kong calligraphy master had a Jian hanging on his studio wall, though he told me he did not know how to use it.

As was the case in Europe and Japan, would-be swordsmen could either seek instruction in the military, or from private schools or individuals. Military instruction tended (and still tends) to be more regimented and done in large groups. In January 2001, while in the grounds of Changsha museum (which houses the fascinating

Han-dynasty tomb findings at Ma Wang Dui), I witnessed a platoon of Public Security officers training in self-defence. This consisted mainly of jabs and hooks combined with high kicks. The riot training that I received in the Royal Hong Kong Police Training School was similarly basic, though effective against a mob.

This type of training is purely utilitarian and, being bereft of any artistic/aesthetic content, cannot be called martial arts; it is merely crude fighting. Chinese society has long had the dual concepts of Wen-Wu: the literary/civil and the martial/military. Many Chinese also practise martial arts in this way, training only in forms (whether external or internal) for health and strength, or for competition to train the intent and spirit; at another extreme, some Chinese (mainly the police/army) practise like our Public Security friends only for use in self-defence. Indeed, there is the Chinese character *Bin*, which is a combination of *Wen* (meaning cultural) and *Wu* (meaning military). This composite character means 'ornamental' and 'practical' combined and, by extension, 'balanced'.

As is the case with karate, many practitioners of Chinese martial arts are turning diamonds into coal, because either they don't know the applications of techniques found in the forms or they know applications that won't work; they do not know the fundamental truth that all forms come from techniques – the techniques do not come from the forms. This is true of all martial arts, with or without weapons. There are other problems too, which cause much of value in Chinese martial arts to remain hidden. The impressive North Chinese internal martial artist Zhai Hua once told me that, while living in China, she and her father tried to practise unobtrusively, because they were often accosted by police who would ask to see if her fists were as fast as their bullets.

Weapons training

How do we become skilled with weapons? In 2001, at a nine-day Tai Chi pushing hands event in Hanover, Giles Busk — a teacher of Cheng Man-ching-style Tai Chi — told me that he was impressed by the directness of the thrusts in my sword demonstration. This kind of focus is trained largely in Tai Chi Neigong and also to a high degree in the spear applications. You need strength to train with weapons, and weapon training in turn gives strength. This is one of the reasons why, in many internal Chinese martial-arts schools, we train with heavy weapons that we would not normally want to use in a real situation. Furthermore, forms may be practised with a spear, sabre or sword, but in actuality one might be using another weapon entirely, such as a mace, axe or stick.

An oft-neglected aspect of swordsmanship is both sword-drawing and preventing sword-drawing. Usually applications are practised with the weapon already in the hand, but this is not a practical way to go through life. On a short journey or at home a Chinese might wear a weapon at the waist, but on longer journeys he would sling it across his back, for ease of walking. Therefore, just as with bare-handed fighting in Tai Chi and other Chinese martial arts there are pre-emptive strikes and jamming techniques to prevent the opponent even launching his attack, so there are similar techniques to trap the opponent's weapon-drawing arm, while simultaneously drawing your own weapon and cutting or striking him with the butt in one movement.

The mythology of the sword from movies (both Western and Chinese) is of a chivalric code, where we draw our weapons, salute and fight. We see the same thing in ludicrous Western gunfights, when the reality was often one of shooting in the back and drawing on unarmed men.

The Chinese, since well before the Tang dynasty, were used to sitting on stools, chairs and benches while eating or drinking, whereas even today the Japanese are more used to sitting or kneeling on tatami mats. This is one of the reasons for the differences in approach in both the unarmed and armed martial arts. It is also clear that what will work in a well-lit, spacious, matted gym may have to be severely adapted for use in a restaurant or back alley.

In weapons training, the same process is necessary as in empty-hand training. The first thing is to train in drills and forms and individual techniques, so that you develop a degree of experience and insight into the essential nature of individual weapons in attack and defence. After a certain amount of practice a degree of mastery is achieved, in that it becomes increasingly possible for you to achieve the perfect result. The final stage is to practise until there is no technique and you can be instantaneous and decisive in any situation.

This final stage is what Chan (Japanese, Zen) Buddhism is about: losing your attachment to the material world and becoming detached. In Taoism it is the stage of 'no me, no you', where Heaven, Earth and Humanity harmonize as one. Practically we become one with the sword, or whatever other weapon we might be using. Both Chinese Youxia (errant knights) and Japanese Samurai found such concepts useful in developing spontaneity in action – something beyond technique.

In his wonderful book *The Lone Samurai* the excellent William Scott Wilson quotes a Chinese calligrapher: 'When the heart [mind] is correct, then the brush is correct.' So it is with weapons. This quote brings to mind the concept of being centrally correct, referred to in the Tai Chi Chuan Classics. The subject of Wilson's book, the swordsman Miyamoto Musashi, is quoted as saying, 'The true Way of swordsmanship is to fight with your opponent and win.'

These concepts of correct mind and the Way were largely the result of the influence of Chan Buddhism, which many swordsmen (including Musashi) took up. Chan embodies contemplation and meditation, which were necessary to develop detachment and the ability to respond spontaneously in any given situation – important qualities in a swordsman.

Musashi told students to 'practise in the morning, train in the evening' and 'temper yourself with 1,000 days of practice and refine yourself with 10,000 days of training'. This is reminiscent of Laozi, who said that a journey of 1,000 Li (Chinese kilometres) starts beneath your feet; and to the reference in the Tai Chi Classics about Li (strength) being like 100-times-refined steel.

The Chinese are prisoners of their history and culture more so than we in the West. In Confucian tradition, social superiors such as teachers are only to be obeyed, but never questioned, and so there are many unspoken assumptions. This holds true of weapon training. In many Chinese styles where applications are taught, it is on the basis of empty hands against empty hands, sword against sword, spear against spear, sabre broadsword against staff or sabre/broadsword. Training to give or receive left-handed attacks is almost unknown. I prefer to train all the permutations.

I recommend training weapon forms and applications in Mirror Form (that is, on the other side) and practising applications against left-handed attacks also, as you cannot choose your opponents. First, Mirror Forms are fun; you really have to relearn the form. Second, this develops both sides of the body. Third, it is of real practical value if one hand is injured or trapped. Indeed, one of my former students, Aidan Cochrane, went into a combat Escrima (Filipino martial-arts) tournament some years ago, for his own amusement and experience, and was able in the second round of one contest to use his left hand and to rest his right for the third round, thus winning the bout. He became a world champion in this type of fighting.

When I taught self-defence to security guards, in the final session I would match them for about 30 seconds against a colleague with a rubber knife; though some were experienced martial artists, barely one in a hundred managed to get by without being slashed or stabbed. My own master had a number of nasty scars on his face and body from knives and Dao, after being attacked by more than one-armed assailants.

Dr Konstantin V. Asmolov from the Russian Academy of Sciences in Moscow told me that in the traditional Korean sword-fighting that he performs, weapon applications are practised against unarmed as well as armed opponents, and weapons techniques are taught before hand techniques. This makes a lot of sense, but problems arise when people lack the emotional maturity and moral qualities to judge whether or not to use a weapon. In many European cultures it is normal to carry a knife: in the Balkans, in Finland, in Scotland. The problem with carrying one is that there is the temptation to use it, especially when faced with a stronger opponent or even multiple opponents.

One factor of crucial importance, apart from the relative skill of two opponents, is the actual quality of the weapons being used. As was the case in Europe, where swordsmen sought blades of Toledo or Damascus steel, in China swordsmen sought to acquire 'precious' weapons. One of the highlights in the film *Crouching Tiger, Hidden Dragon* is the scene in a Wu Guan where Michelle Yeoh, though the better martial artist, sees one weapon after another broken by Zhang Ziyi's magic sword. Combat weapons of quality were often embellished with motifs such as the seven stars of Ursa Major, dragons and phoenixes and seal calligraphy (a highly stylized form of writing). Throughout Chinese history, weapons could also have a ritual function and would not necessarily be designed for combat.

Three Tai Chi weapons

As the three most common Tai Chi weapons are the Dao (sabre/broadsword), Jian (straight sword) and Qiang (spear), I will discuss these in turn in some detail. The traditional saying in Chinese martial arts about the degree of difficulty of these three is: 'Qiang – one hundred days; Dao – one thousand days, Jian – ten thousand days'. Personally, I think the Qiang is a lot more difficult than that.

All three weapons share certain characteristics; all three can be substituted by everyday objects, such as sticks, umbrellas or even (in the case of Dao and Jian) rolled-up newspapers. In many Chinese martial arts there are names that are literary allusions for each technique (one technique may be a movement such as a stab, or a complex series of moves); this acts as a kind of shorthand for the initiated, as well as being an interesting and amusing way (if you understand the allusion) of remembering the technique.

There are particular techniques or tactics for each of these weapons; beyond this we combine applications with the appropriate footwork. As with empty-hand techniques we have the usual permutations of in and out, up and down, left and right, Yin and Yang, orthodox and reverse, closing and opening, and so on. One great fault of many weapon practitioners is to think only of the weapon; there are in fact many important movements in weapon forms with the free hand, the feet and body.

There are two-handed applications with the Dao and the Jian; this can be useful in giving greater control over the weapon, particularly when faced with a powerful opponent or one who has a heavy weapon such as a Guan Dao. However, in most applications one hand is used to grip the handle, while the other is used to support the weapon, to grab the opponent or the opponent's weapon, to lock or disarm him, to push the opponent away or to pull him into a technique. The feet and knees are used to kick the opponent when our weapon is occupied in controlling the opponent's weapon or where, for example, a Tan (upward slash) technique such as 'Searching the Sea' (from the sabre form that I teach) is blocked and we follow up with an immediate kick. Additionally, kicks to the opponent's weapon or weapon hand can make him lose control of his weapon. Many weapon applications can also be adapted to empty-hand fighting and vice versa.

The grip of the weapon changes, too; when in an on-guard position, the grip should be light, but generally we tighten the grip whenever impacting our weapon with either the opponent or his weapon. For Dao and Jian, you generally have a better control of the weapon if the hand is closer to the guard; however, you can extend the range of the weapon by gripping it nearer the butt.

The Chinese had widely available drill manuals written by military experts, such as the famous General Qi Jiguang's *Ji Xiao Xin Shu* (*New Book Examining the Records*). As well as containing his *Classic of Boxing*, which only deals with empty-hand techniques, the book also includes training with long weapons such as spear and halberd and Dao and shield, listing the techniques and strategies to be practised. It should also be appreciated that weapons did not (and do not) exist in a vacuum and some were developed or altered to deal with likely opponents, such as Japanese pirates or nomadic horsemen. As well as such military manuals, there were the techniques and strategies peculiar to particular styles and schools of Chinese martial arts, which for obvious reasons were not always widely known outside that school. Sometimes they might be included in the manuals of a particular school, which were available only to advanced students or were only taught orally.

I will now deal with the three classical Chinese martial-arts and Tai Chi weapons individually.

The Dao

'Dao' is often translated as sabre or broadsword, but in fact any single-edged cutting weapon of whatever length can be classified as a Dao. I will confine my discussion to the single Dao, which is the most common version used in Chinese martial arts. The length depends on the size of the practitioner, but normally when the handle is gripped, it should be possible to touch the ground with the tip. The Dao was the weapon of choice for the foot soldier, convoy escort and bandit, because it was cheap to make, comparatively easy to use and extremely versatile, particularly at close quarters. The techniques can be adapted for use with a stick or rolled-up newspaper, or even with bare hands.

The Dao was supposedly invented by the Yellow Emperor (traditionally c. 2698–2598 BCE), who is also credited with writing a classic on medicine. The god of the Dao is Cang Er and it is identified with the tiger, so stances are long and low, with much crouching, leaping and slashing. However, as is normal in Tai Chi, there are techniques where 'tiger' refers to the opponent and others where we are the tiger.

The particular Tai Chi Dao form that I practise is called Xuan Xuan Dao. *Xuan* means 'dark', 'mysterious' or 'profound', and 'Xuan Xuan' was the Taoist name for Zhang Sanfeng, who is credited with being the founder of Tai Chi. The famous Tai Chi historian Wu Tu-nan published a book on this form around 1930, although his version of the form differs from mine in some details.

There are two main types of the single Dao in Tai Chi: the more common one broadens out from the handle and is leaf- or fish-shaped when placed flat, while the other is more like the Japanese katana, and so can be more easily used to stab, although it is not as easy to support it with the free hand. In both cases coloured ribbon or cloth is usually tied to the butt of the weapon. There are various debates about what this was used for; I believe it was simply to wipe off sweat or blood from the hands, or possibly to wrap around the hand as a safety measure so that you wouldn't lose the weapon when you impacted with something or someone.

THE EIGHT MAJOR WAYS OF USING THE DAO:

These are essentially the orthodox techniques. In addition, the butt of the Dao could be used for striking vital points at close quarters; the blunt edge could be used when it was inappropriate to cause permanent injury with the sharpened edge, or to avoid impacting on the opponent's weapon with the sharp edge and thus damaging it; the flat of the blade could be used to bounce or slap the opponent's weapon or arm out of the way; and so on. There are techniques that are, or can be, precautionary, as when we entwine the Dao around the body in 'Turn Around Hiding the Sabre', to protect the neck, back and legs when we turn.

The Dao is a close- to medium-range weapon and is therefore most versatile; because only one edge is sharp, the other one can be supported by the free hand, or the blunt edge can be wrapped round the body while slashing in different directions. This range also means that there are many Qinna (seizing and holding) and kicking techniques in Tai Chi Dao; indeed, many practitioners neglect the use of the free hand, whether in attack or defence, and become fixated on their own and their opponents' weapons.

The names of the Dao techniques contain many cultural allusions:

● For example, there is 'Sparrowhawk Turning Round', followed by 'Peng Spreading Its Wings' – a reference to the gigantic mythical bird of the philosopher Zhuangzi, which could fly 90,000 km (56,000 miles) up into the sky and 60,000 km (37,000 miles) to the Southern Ocean to migrate. The sparrows and cicadas laughed at the Peng, wondering why it could not be like them and simply fly from tree to tree, or even just from branch to branch. Zhuangzi's point was that we need to be true to our own nature. If you are a gigantic bird, then you need to behave like one and not like a sparrow or a cicada. This indicates that the eponymous Dao techniques should be small and contracting and large and expansive respectively.

● The technique 'Taking Off the Boots While Drunk' refers to an incident involving the poet Li Bai. One time, when he was a favourite of the Emperor, he was drunk in the imperial court and ordered Gao Lishi, an influential eunuch, to take off his boots and thus made an enemy for life.

● 'Embrace the Moon' alludes to another Li Bai story. One night while on a boat on the River Yangzi, he was drinking and chanting poetry about the beauty of the moon's reflection on the water. He was so overcome with emotion that he reached overboard to embrace the moon on the water and fell in and drowned. When doing this technique the body should therefore be bent well forward, as if about to fall over.

When I was in the Royal Hong Kong Police Training School we were taught to use the long baton and rattan shield for riot control. As with basic Dao strikes, we would advance with the baton and forehand-strike, backhand-strike, thrust and hit with the shield, repeating until there was no one left to hit. This is crude but effective against a crowd, although it is unlikely to trouble a skilled swordsman when it comes to one-on-one combat. As was the case with European swordsmanship, a convoy escort or common soldier was unlikely to be any match for a trained Youxia (errant knight), who theoretically at least had spent years perfecting his skills under top-level masters.

How effective is the Dao? The leaf- or fish-shaped Dao is not very effective for stabbing, as its design prevents effective penetration. And the guard is purely functional and not suitable for trapping an opponent's blade. Even in chopping there are drawbacks. On a number of occasions, while working as a detective inspector in the Criminal Investigation Department of the Royal Hong Kong Police, I saw victims of gangland choppings who had been attacked with either Kung Fu Dao or with butchers' cleavers. While in some cases fingers or limbs were at least partially severed, some 'victims' had received multiple chop wounds to the head and back, but were still able to walk around and function more or less normally. The best targets for the Dao would seem to be sensitive areas such as the face, joints and bones.

1 Pi *To chop/split from various angles*

2 Ci *To stab/pierce*

3 **Tan** *To search, slashing upwards to the groin*

4 **Tuo** *To push up, using the free hand to support the back of the blade*

5 **Ti** *To raise/lift the sabre, usually with the sharp edge facing up*

Liao *To stir (for example, a diversion and slash in a continuous movement)*

7 Chen *To sink, using the sabre to press down on the opponent's weapon or body*

8 Lu *The sideways use of force, as in diverting an attack to the side*

Turn Around Hiding the Sabre

Sparrowhawk Turning Around

Peng – Spreading its Wings

Taking off the Boots While Drunk

Embrace the Moon

The Qiang

The second classical Chinese martial-arts weapon used in Tai Chi is the Qiang or spear. A spear is really a staff with a metal head stuck on at least one end, for stabbing, cutting and/or hooking, depending on the type of head that is used. Of course the origin lies in the pointed sticks used for fighting and hunting by our forefathers, and some Qiang (especially the lighter versions) were also used as javelins – the drawback being that, as well as throwing away your weapon, it could also be used against you, by its intended target. I have not come across references in modern Chinese martial-arts practice to the throwing of spears, and I suspect this was almost exclusively a military and hunting use of the weapon.

Various types of spear can be found in the hands of deities such as Tai Gong Bing Fa (Supreme Lord of Military Affairs). But more importantly, when using the spear, the spirit is that of the dragon – an unpredictable and enigmatic character – and so there is much soaring and plunging, spiralling and thrusting.

There are two characters for *Qiang*, one with the radical (root character which gives a clue to the meaning of a Chinese character) for 'metal' and the other with the radical for 'wood'. Though a Qiang could theoretically be all-wood or all-metal, more usually in Chinese martial arts it consisted of a wooden body that tapered towards a metal head. This tapering was designed to make thrusting more efficacious and to make the business end more flexible, so that you could use the spear to bounce away the attacks of an opponent, forcing him to lose control of his weapon and thus also bouncing into a counter-attacking thrust. However, the excessive whippiness of modern Wushu spears is unsuitable for this.

The length of the spear can vary somewhat; this is partly dictated by the height and strength of the exponent. However, when training in Hong Kong we practised the spear form and drills with much longer (up to 3 m/10 ft) and therefore heavier spears than the ones we used for applications, which would normally be less than 2 m (6½ ft) long. At a meeting of the Hong Kong Chinese Martial Arts Association,

which I attended in the mid-1970s, the consensus was that a gent's umbrella was better suited to be employed as a spear than as a sword or sabre, as there was much greater control in defence and power in thrusting when using spear techniques.

A common drill is 'sticking' or 'entwining spears', whereby two exponents cross spears and walk in clockwise and anti-clockwise circles, while maintaining contact with the crossed spears and then circling them clockwise and anti-clockwise; in effect this is a kind of pushing hands with spears, and is also useful in building basic arm and leg strength, as well as in training to unbalance the opponent and trap his spear.

The greatest advantage of the spear – its length – is also its greatest weakness. In Tai Chi spear strategy, the object is usually to keep the opponent at the point of the spear, although once the spear is seized or when a swordsman steps inside its range, the spearman is at a disadvantage. At close quarters the feet, butt, rear hand and body of the weapon are used in defence or attack, and the spearman might have to let go of his weapon with one or both hands so that he can close with, and strike or grapple with, his opponent. In medieval European weapon manuals there are many examples of this tactic. Even possession of a (normally) two-handed weapon such as the spear did not obviate the necessity to acquire empty-handed skills.

There are various on-guard positions with the spear, as with the other weapons, but in most of them the point is kept towards the opponent. In the Celtic tradition, entering a strange land with the spear pointing forward was a declaration of war, but carrying it on the shoulder was a token of friendship. I doubt the shades of the great Chinese spear masters of former times would argue with this.

In *Ji Xiao Xin Shu* (*New Book Examining the Records*), attributed to the Ming-dynasty General Qi Jiguang (1528–87), some techniques have purely functional names, such as 'Low Thrust Technique', while others borrow names from Chinese history and myth, such as 'Running Horse Turning Its Head' (from a story about Qin Shi Huangdi, the first Chinese emperor, who went to Tai Shan to present offerings to the gods), or even from literature, such as 'Black-Eared Kite Flies, Fish Leaps' (from the *Book of Odes*, also quoted in Mencius).

The principles of using the spear include adhering, connecting, entwining and stabbing; lifting and hitting, dragging and dotting, often using the opponent's weapon to unbalance him or as a platform to bounce into a thrust, thus making attack out of defence.

THERE ARE EIGHT MAJOR WAYS OF USING THE QIANG:

These are essentially the orthodox techniques. The first four are the warp (vertical and horizontal); the latter four are the woof (diagonal). In addition, the butt and body of the Qiang could be used for striking and pushing; one or both hands could disengage and/or the feet could be used at close quarters. The spear could also be used horizontally to push and pull back an opponent or a group of people.

Altogether, the spear is a great weapon for developing focus and learning how to use total body force. When thrusting, the front index finger should point to the target. First, this helps to develop focus and gives added control; and second, the extended index finger prevents the front hand and thumb from being put out of action if the opponent has a bladed weapon (although the index finger won't be feeling too clever).

It is a great pity that so many Tai Chi practitioners never learn the use of the spear. I have taught it to more than one thousand students over the years, but only a handful are able to demonstrate the combination of power and precision that is required. Regular practice of Neigong is essential for quality spear-play.

1 Peng *Use of force in an upward direction*

2 Lu *Use of force to either side*

3 Ji *Use of force straight and to the front*

4 **An** *Use of force in a downward direction*

5 **Tiao** *To lift or stir up, usually exposing the opponent's body, head or limbs for a counter-attack, by coming up underneath his weapon*

6 **Tan** *To rebound; that is, off the opponent's weapon into a thrust or strike, simultaneously making him lose his grip on, or control over, his weapon*

7 **Qian** *To literally drag/pull; thus spiralling or entwining the spear, causing the opponent to lose balance or lose control of his weapon*

8 **Dian** *To dot or thrust with a staff or the unbladed end of a spear, focusing all the force on just one point*

The Jian

Let us now look at what is considered to be the most subtle of the Chinese martial-arts weapons, the Jian or double-edged sword. The character for 'sword' sounds the same and is similar, except for the radical to the character *Jian*, which means 'to examine' (with a view to avoiding possible danger). The spirit of the Jian is that of the dragon, being enigmatic and versatile, able to coil and uncoil, soar and plunge. It is important that we become one with the sword, which is then the dragon, not the sword alone. The same applies when we are using the spear, which is also identified with the dragon, and when using the sabre, which is identified with the tiger.

In Chinese history there were three types of swordsmen. First, there were the Sword Immortals, 'Jian Xian', such as Lu Tongpin of Eight Immortals fame; Li Bai, the famous Tang-dynasty poet and drinker; Xu Jingming and others whose swordsmanship was used for supernatural purposes such as exorcism. Then there were the Sword Knights or Paladin, 'Jian Xia', men such as Jing Ke, who almost succeeded in his fatal attempt in the third century BCE to assassinate the cruel and tyrannical Qin Shi Huangdi, but died from the seven thrusts he received from that bloody emperor; Nie Zheng and others, who were thought to exhibit the quality (still considered important today in Chinese martial arts) of 'Yi Qi', which is a combination of righteousness and loyalty, and whose swordsmanship was used to avenge wrongs. Li Bai also belongs to this group; he once wrote, 'At 15 I loved the sword', and during his wanderings he behaved as a Paladin and killed unrighteous men with his sword. Finally there were the Sword Guests or 'Jian Ke', such as Hong Quan, Nie Yin Liang and Gong Sun Da Liang (the last two were female), whose sword practice was purely for fun.

There are fabulous stories about the Sword Immortals' abilities, while the Paladin used their swords in private quarrels, like Western gunslingers (good and bad), in what was the Wild East, and the Sword Guests tended to use the sword in play. There were also – as with other weapons, and as in Europe – training manuals on the sword during the Ming dynasty, such as the 'Chao Xian Double-handed Sword'.

God of Literature –

Raising the Wine Vessel

In ancient times there were many famous swordsmiths, such as Gan Jiang from the kingdom of Wu (c. 300 BCE), whose steel swords were considered supernatural, because of their superiority in sharpness and flexibility compared to the bronze weapons used by the military. Obviously superior weapons were more expensive and therefore much rarer. Well-known makes of sword include Dragon Well (originally from Henan Province, but now made all over China) and Seven Stars swords. You can also now buy Shaolin swords at the Northern Shaolin Temple, at vastly inflated prices; they are no better than those sold much more cheaply elsewhere, but the name 'Shaolin' is embossed on them.

The god of the Jian was Fei Yang, but I have been unable to find out much about this gentleman. There were male and female Jian, as there were male and female Dao, and often supernatural qualities were ascribed to them; thus some swords were thought to be able to transform themselves into dragons, and there were cases of human sacrifice to honour certain prized swords. The length of the Jian varied considerably, from swords that could be hidden up the sleeve, to the relatively short bronze swords of the Zhou dynasty (c. 1100–221 BCE) and swords that, like European long swords, could be as much as 2 m (7 ft) in length.

In Buddhism the sword is the symbol of wisdom and penetrating insight and, when wielded by a god, it cuts away all doubts and perplexities to clear the way for knowledge of the truth. Taoists viewed the sword as the symbol of victory over evil and it was wielded by deities such as Zhong Kui, who uses it to slay ghosts, and Lu Tungpin, who used it on his travels to subdue demonic forces. My own Tai Chi sword form contains the technique 'God of Literature Raising the Wine Vessel'; and many swords are decorated with the Seven Star motif that is emblematic of Ursa Major (the Great Bear), also known as The Plough and the abode of said god. He is often depicted standing on a fish, as the carp in the Yellow River was said to swim upstream. Carps, which passed through the Dragon Gate (Longmen), were said to transform into dragons. Dragon Gate is the name of one of the main schools of Taoism, and there are references to both fish and dragons in the sword and sabre forms that I teach.

There are dozens of different sword forms in Chinese martial arts; my Chinese martial-arts encyclopaedia lists five forms from Wudang Mountain alone. In Tai Chi there are also many different sword forms. In the Wu style there is a double sword form, though this is a modern invention (from the last 50 years), while the Hao style has a form using a short sword. The sword form that I practise is very similar to the one shown in Wu Tunan's book on the Tai Chi sword. Wu states that another name for this form is 'Heaven and Earth Sword' (Qian Kun Jian – this can also be translated as 'Male and Female Sword'). In the *Book of Changes*, Qian is the hexagram for Heaven and therefore represents the supreme male principle or Yang, while Kun is the hexagram for Earth and therefore represents the supreme female principle or Yin. Indeed, this is the essence of the Tai Chi sword form, combining the slow and the fast, the hard and the soft, expanding and contracting, soaring and plunging.

Wu's book often gives the sword applications as being against a spear rather than, as is more common, against another sword. In fact many of the techniques can be adapted equally well for either situation.

Let us now consider the different parts that make up the Jian. First, and perhaps most important, is its double-edged blade. It is wider, thicker and therefore less sharp at the guard than other swords, and it tapers to the point and often also to both edges; its length and thickness are in proportion to one another. This means that the upper part of the blade is mainly used defensively, to impact with the opponent's weapon, while the lower part is used to slice and stab the opponent.

The handle and scabbard might be plain and made of the same material as the sword, but often they were made of wood and covered with decorations such as snakeskin and precious and semi-precious stones such as jade. There were also famous Jian, which could take more than a hundred days to make. There is a reference in the Tai Chi Classic *Interpretation of the Practice of the Thirteen Tactics* to 'Moving the Jin [dynamic and skilled force used in Tai Chi Chuan] like 100-times-refined steel'. In the same way, such swords were refined to remove impurities and therefore make them more reliable.

Golden Needle Pointing South

Male and Female Phoenix Spreading Their Wings

Most Chinese martial-arts (as opposed to purely military) swords have a tassel attached to the butt. There is some debate about what this was used for; some people even practise in such a way as to keep the tassel swinging freely. This may be interesting and fun, but it is fundamentally ridiculous; to use a famous analogy, we should be concentrating on the moon, not on the finger that points to it. The tassel was simply to wipe off sweat or blood from the hands, or to wrap around the hand as a safety measure so that you wouldn't lose the weapon when you impacted with something or someone.

It is difficult to write about Chinese swordsmanship without mentioning Miyamoto Musashi (1584–1645), the famous Japanese swordsman. Japan, like China, was (and is) a Confucian and ordered society; there was a certain way to do things. For example, in traditional Chinese and Japanese society the concept of left-handedness did not exist. Chopsticks, writing brushes and swords were all controlled by the right hand. It was a matter of fitting in. Someone using chopsticks with his left hand would make the right-handed neighbour on his left feel uncomfortable. And the nature of Chinese calligraphy requires that the strokes that make up Chinese characters are written in a certain order by a right-handed person; while drilling a class or a military unit it is highly divisive and troublesome to have someone using the 'wrong' hand. Elsewhere in this book I called my teacher a maverick Chinaman – this is partly because he was unashamedly left-handed, and highly effective with it.

In the sword form that I practise, the sword is passed from left hand to right and back again six times; additionally there are some double-handed techniques. It was only when reading a translation of Hans Talhoffer's sword-fighting and close-quarter combat manual of 1467 that I encountered such tactics in another sword tradition. This book clearly shows that European and Chinese martial arts were contemporaneously developing along similar lines more than five hundred years ago. Other European tactics included holding the long sword blade with the left hand, thus almost turning it into a spear (often a bit of leather that could slide up and down was attached to the blade for this purpose); and, once you had closed with an armed opponent, dropping your own weapon to strike, stab with a dagger or grapple with him.

Even amid all this accepted order that pervaded Chinese and Japanese society certain maverick spirits made their own order. Musashi was of this breed. He killed his first Samurai at the age of 13 by throwing him to the ground and beating him on the head with a stick until he died. Later he was to defeat Samurai with wooden swords, an oar and even a bow. The use of wooden weapons is not strange, for good wood is better than bad metal. There was at least one incident in which Musashi used a wooden sword to break his opponent's metal sword in two. And I have witnessed a solid metal Chinese broadsword snap in two under the impact from a staff on its sharp edge. As with Tai Chi bare-handed techniques, using force against force is a poor way to defend yourself.

Let us now deal with the names of sword techniques:

● Logically speaking, if we are doing the form outdoors at daybreak, we should start off facing west, with the rising sun at our backs, because fairly early on we have 'Golden Needle Pointing South' on the left-hand side. The poetic nature of certain cultural references in the names of techniques helps us to remember the sequence and to better understand the eponymous technique.

● In 'Male and Female Phoenix Spreading Their Wings' the sword hand and the free hand make simultaneous and equally large intersecting circles, one soaring, one swooping.

● 'Li Guang Shooting an Arrow at the Tiger' requires us to draw back the sword at shoulder, level like a bow and arrow, before firing it with maximum power to pierce the hide of the tiger (your enemy). Li Bai refers to him in the poem 'Horses of the North': 'Who now pities fast-moving Li Guang of Han ...?'

There is also a story that goes with the technique. Li Guang (died 119 BCE), nicknamed 'the Flying General', was travelling on one occasion in dark night when he thought he saw a tiger on the mountainside, so he drew his bow and fired an arrow at

Li Guang Drawing the Bow to Shoot an Arrow at the Tiger

Fisherman Casting his Net

it. The next morning he found the arrow embedded in a rock shaped like a tiger. This story is about intent; only because he was shooting a tiger was he able to pierce the rock. In the Wu family this technique is called 'Li Guang Shooting an Arrow at the Rock'.

● 'Fisherman Casting His Net' is an expansive movement, where both arms are flung upwards and out, while the front leg is raised; it can be used against two opponents, simultaneously kicking one, while parrying or cutting the other.

● 'Pei Gong Cleaving a Snake' is a reference to an incident that occurred one night when Pei Gong – the courtesy title of Liu Pang (247–195 BCE), first emperor of the Han dynasty – was a village headman, when he sliced into bits a large snake that threatened some villagers. In the sword form, when doing this technique, we retract in what is a defensive technique, then pull the sword and front leg up, in what can be an offensive or defensive technique (all this resembles pulling back to draw the sword from its scabbard), before slashing the opponent's leg.

● 'Tai Gong [Great-Grandfather] Fishing' refers to a story about Jiang Shang of the Western Zhou dynasty (1100–771 BCE). He is supposed to have spent years fishing on the banks of the Weishui River in Shaanxi, often dangling his line in mid-air without hook or bait, claiming that he was waiting to catch a virtuous ruler. In his eighties he was finally made Prime Minister by King Wen.

Next, let us look at the technicalities of Tai Chi swordplay. The principles of using the spear include adhering, connecting, entwining and stabbing; lifting and hitting, dragging and dotting, often using the opponent's weapon to unbalance him, or as a platform to bounce into a thrust, thus making attack out of defence. Though the range is somewhat different, we can use all of these skills with the sword too.

Pei Gung Cleaving a Snake

Great-Grandfather Fishing

Spin Around to Rein in the Horse

Hanging the Golden Bell Upside Down

Spin Around and Sweep Across

THERE ARE EIGHT MAJOR WAYS OF USING THE JIAN:

I should also mention that, unlike the Dao, the Jian should not be used to cut over the crown of our own head. This is not because (as one Tai Chi book has it) we would thereby sever our contact with Heaven and no longer have the much-beloved 'suspended head-top', but because it is simply dangerous to have a double-edged weapon passing over the crown of the head in this way, for any misjudgement or impact with the opponent's weapon at this point might result in us being cut with our own weapon.

The unreliability of weapons means that great emphasis must be given to footwork and body evasion, and we should try to avoid direct hard impact with the opponent's weapon. The grip should be light, but should tighten when impacting with the opponent's weapon or body.

The use of the free hand in Chinese swordplay is – as far as I'm aware – unique, because the index and middle fingers are extended and kept close together, while the other fingers are bent. In techniques such as 'Rhinoceros Facing the Moon' (Wu Tu-nan calls this 'Seven Stars Style') and 'Spin to Rein in the Horse' the sword tip points to the tips of the extended fingers of the free hand. In techniques such as 'God of Literature Raising the Wine Vessel' and 'Hanging the Golden Bell Upside Down' the two fingers form a triangle with the sword tip and the raised foot. In 'Shooting Star Chasing the Moon' and 'Spin and Sweep Across' the free hand acts as a counterpoint to the sword, facing up if the sword hand is palm down and vice versa.

On a more practical basis, the free hand was held in this sword-like two-fingered manner because it also facilitates the use of Dim Mak thrusts with the fingers to vital areas of the opponent's body, or gripping and closing, or tearing veins, arteries and pressure points. Instead of holding the free hand in this way, we could equally well hold a poniard (short dagger) or buckler. 'Poniard' is an interesting word and comes from the medieval French *poignard*, which in turn comes from the French *poing*, meaning a fist. In Tai Chi there is a specific method of pushing hands called Zhou Lu, which is practised with the fists clenched. This is designed both to make it second nature to grapple with clenched fists when holding something light and to use pushing hands skills to control or cut with a weapon when at close quarters with an opponent. As with the other weapons, the feet could be used in defence or attack, including specific kicks to the opponent's sword hand to disarm him.

On a more spiritual note, according to Eva Wong in her excellent book *The Shambhala Guide to Taoism*, the sword-hand mudra (hand gesture) with the command 'destroy' was the final one in a series of ten mudras and commands that were designed to dispel malevolent spirits.

1 **Kan** *To chop or slice, usually diagonally downwards*

2 **Liao** *To stir; for example, diverting and slashing in one continuous movement*

3 **Mo** *To stroke or rub; as in a subtle, circular diversion or a delicate slice*

4 **Ci** *To stab or pierce in any direction; usually the flat of the blade is horizontal when stabbing the body, to allow it to penetrate the ribs*

5 Qian *To draw forth, as in an upward diversion, using a whipping action*

6 **Dian** *To raise the sword, as in a defensive or counter-offensive change of guard; indeed, many techniques are specifically designed for application with a change from left to right high guards or vice versa (such as 'Bamboo Basket on the Left and Right' and 'Swift Bird Darting Through the Forest')*

7 **Heng** *To sweep across in a horizontal diversion or attack; this is often followed by a thrust*

8 **Dao** *To invert the sword, so that the butt of the guard is up and the point down; this can be used in a sideways or upward-directed diversion or slice*

Chapter 5

Masters and Students

True transmission

In Chinese arts, including Tai Chi, true transmission is essential to enable the living art to survive. Only what the Taoist philosopher Zhuangzi (c. 369–286 BCE) called a 'true person' can give true transmission. A true person is someone who has acquired the skill and experience in a lineage of true transmission, so that he or she can pass on the art to later generations. It is my aim in this section of the book to look at aspects that affect true transmission.

Back in 1975 George Button, Chief Physical Training Instructor at the Royal Hong Kong Police Training School, said that if I wanted to learn Tai Chi seriously, I should go and see his old Sifu, Cheng Tin-hung. George was a top-level Aikido master and self-defence expert, so his recommendation was good enough for me.

In Chinese martial arts, including Tai Chi, the master–disciple relationship is vital if there is to be a true transmission of the art; there has to be a chemistry, or karmic connection, between the individuals concerned. Largely thanks to George, I had this connection with Cheng Tin-hung from the beginning.

In Chinese, *Yuan Fen* means the appointed lot by which people are brought together, or a predestined relationship. By itself *Yuan* means cause / connection / relationship, while *Fen* is a share / duty or to divide / distinguish, so I guess you can have both, either or neither at any one time, with any person / persons and thing / things. Karma is similar – essentially, it means actions that produce effects at another stage, time and / or place of existence. I had both *Yuan Fen* – his second wife said I was like a son to him – and an ever-changing karma with Sifu Cheng. The karma continues today with these writings.

The Life of Marpa the Translator, translated from a Tibetan work written in the early 16th century by the so-called 'mad yogin' Tsang Nyon Heruka (yogin is another term for a yoga master), contains many curious tales about the master–disciple relationship. Marpa was an 11th-century Tibetan farmer, scholar and teacher, who travelled to India three times to study Buddhism. The characters of Tsang and Marpa are very different from the stereotypical Buddhist sage.

For example, one of Marpa's disciples says to him, 'You said that if one does not enjoy meat, liquor and women, it is a disservice to oneself. It appears to us that this is no different from what we do.' Marpa replies, 'Though I enjoy sense pleasures, I am not fettered by them.'

Outwardly Marpa did not resemble a spiritual person; he did not wear the robes of a monk or yogin; he did not seem to spend a lot of time meditating or in retreat. He said, 'Although everyone attains enlightenment by meditating, if one becomes enlightened without effort in meditation, that is it.'

Marpa's master wrote of seven yogas, consisting of eating food, wearing clothes, sleeping, walking, talking, bathing and making offerings. We all do most of these, but how many of us actually think about what we are doing?

In these arts, as in Chinese martial arts, a student who wishes to be trained in practice that can lead to enlightenment must first make a personal connection with an authentic teacher of the lineage, who has had a true transmission of such practice from his own teacher and thus has the ability and understanding to teach his students in turn. Again, as with Chinese martial arts, the so-called 'inner art' or teachings are rarely written down, but are mainly a one-on-one oral transmission. An authentic teacher will not only know these oral teachings, but will have put them into practice. It is said: 'No guru, no teachings, no path'. The Sanskrit term *guru* literally means 'weighty one' and refers to an enlightened master, although its English meaning is less specific. Obstacles are encountered on the path, which – when overcome – can heighten the student's realization.

On Marpa's final trip to India he found that his teacher had become a wanderer, 'to enter the action' and encounter the world directly. Because of this it took Marpa more than eight months of trials and tribulations to find his teacher. In exactly the same way, Zhang Sanfeng – the so-called 'Filthy Taoist' and founder of Tai Chi Chuan – was not someone who stayed in one place. When I climbed Hengshan, the Southern Sacred Mountain, in Hunan province in 2000 I bought a book in a temple there, which mentioned that Zhang had moved to Hengshan from Wudang Mountain, owing to being constantly disturbed at his Taoistic practice by pilgrims and visitors.

The idea of a personal teaching according to the character of a disciple is interesting. Marpa also said, 'I have to give each son-disciple the appropriate special transmission and activity.' It is not so simple for the would-be disciple, and one of Marpa's gurus remarked about one of Marpa's friends, 'He and I have no karmic connection.' In other words, the friend could never become his disciple.

The same is true in Chinese martial arts. In Baguazhang / 'Eight Diagram Palm', for example, it is well known that the complexity of the system led its founder, Dong Haichuan, to teach his disciples in different ways, according to their characters and body type. In Tai Chi Chuan, Yang Luchan's disciples Ling Shan, Wan Chun and Quan You were famous respectively for striking power, for strength and for footwork and skill in evasion.

Nowadays few people practising martial arts have any meaningful karmic connection with their students, or with their teachers. Many teachers have, to a greater or lesser extent, become supermarkets, and many students are simply shoppers. Few are really dedicated and prepared to make the sacrifices necessary to learn or teach a complete art.

'Mountains high, Emperor far'. Chinese proverb

Students

The word 'student' has a Latin root in the verb *studere*, meaning to be eager or diligent and, by extension, to study. A student may simply be someone engaged in the study of a particular subject or may be someone devoted to learning. Study itself includes examining, analysing, thinking, showing interest and purpose. Yet how many students of Tai Chi actually practise with this attitude?

In Chinese martial arts there are various types of student. First, there is a family structure, so students are classified as Elder/Younger Brothers/Sisters, according to when they started learning from a particular teacher. By the same token, one of your teacher's fellow students would be your Elder/Younger Aunt/Uncle.

A general term for students of a master is Tudi (*tu di*), meaning literally 'younger brothers who are followers'. More succinctly, we can call them apprentices. Students are then divided into inside-the-door and outside-the-door students (see pages 34 and 230). 'Inside-the-door students' are normally referred to as 'door people' or, more properly, 'disciples', because they have undergone a ritual ceremony with their teacher.

In Tai Chi Chuan we undergo this ceremony prior to being taught Neigong. Traditionally, only after the student and teacher had known one another for six years did the teacher offer to teach Neigong, although nowadays the period is usually much shorter, but still long enough for student and teacher to get to know one another properly.

Some teachers expect almost blind obedience from their students. This is not healthy. Of course the student should respect his teacher's greater experience and knowledge, but this should not require him to ape the teacher's every action and opinion. Then again, some students are looking for a guru to direct their every thought and action, rather than for a teacher. This is a path with dangers for both students and teachers alike. It is as bad to question nothing as it is to question everything.

Many people say that the evolution from student to master takes 10, 15 or 20 years. They are all wrong: the measure is not in terms of time, but in terms of ability. My teacher became a full-time professional Tai Chi instructor at the age of 19, after just three years of full-time tuition from Qi Minxuan. I know of other so-called masters who have trained for 20, 30 or even 40 years and who are still, at best, mediocre.

Some say that Tai Chi is more difficult to use than hard-style martial arts. I disagree with regard to the system that I teach, which I believe is easier to learn because the basic techniques are freer as well as more versatile. In particular the defensive techniques are more efficient, and require less physical effort on the part of the student. Also, many martial arts are taught as if the opponent can only come from the same art, or as if he is a complete simpleton. I do not teach in this way.

A GOOD STUDENT:

- **Practises**
- **Looks and listens**
- **Thinks, and then asks**
- **Is neither too harsh nor too soft with his training partners**
- **Constantly seeks to learn, both inside and outside the class**
- **Trains and competes honestly.**

Too many students spend time talking rather than doing. Learn by watching and listening to others – not just the teacher – and learn to discriminate. If in doubt, ask. It is a major weakness of many students that they don't ask questions and, when they do, they ask the wrong question, such as 'What if . . . ?' or 'How do I get out of . . . ?' No teacher can teach you everything, even if they wanted to (which many don't). However, by practising certain basic techniques that follow key principles you will not find it necessary to ask the wrong question so often.

If you know something, then be positive: show that you know it. If you don't know something, then be positive: admit that you don't know it and seek to find it out. When learning something new, analyse it in the light of what you already know and, in turn, use new ideas and information to analyse your old knowledge.

There is no point in bigger and stronger students relying mainly on their strength against smaller opponents. On the other hand, if techniques are not performed properly – perhaps out of a misguided sense of gallantry towards a female opponent, for instance – then the opponent is given a false sense of security.

It is a deplorable trait amongst certain male students to attempt to correct female students of the same (or even greater) experience as themselves. I once saw a male student of six months' experience attempt to correct (wrongly) a female student with three years' experience. However, experienced and capable students do have a responsibility to advise and encourage beginners. They must also accept that they have no divine right to defeat every beginner. It is not enough to turn up at a class once a week and expect the teacher to do everything for you. It is up to you to get the most out of your training in a class, and to work on your own training. This is not just a physical approach, but also includes reading and analysing.

Training should be honest. If you feel you can beat someone, then do so. I have no time for instructors whom I have met in places like Taiwan who, wanting to impress Westerners with their skills and expecting to beat them merely because they have been training for a certain number of years, get angry with those who fail to play the game and allow themselves to be thrown around. In their own way, masters must be students too.

Inspiration

Every teacher needs to give inspiration to his or her students. I readily accept this responsibility, but where is the poor teacher to find inspiration? Although, since 1975, I have only followed one master and have only practised one method, I have had many sources of inspiration.

But what is inspiration? My *Webster's Third International Dictionary* defines it as 'a divine influence or action upon the lives of certain persons that is believed to qualify them to receive and communicate sacred revelation; or the act or power of moving the intellect or emotions'. Let me tell you about some of these 'divine influences or actions' in my own life.

I once said to my master's eldest son that his father was a great teacher. His son said that his father was not a great teacher, but a man of great knowledge and experience. This was closer to the truth. I spent most days from 1975 to 1984 going to my master's house and training on the rooftop. He ran morning and evening sessions, six days per week. When I first went, he was always there and spent most of the classtime on the rooftop. He did not teach a class in a conventional sense; people would simply do their practice singly or in groups, sometimes under the guidance of an Elder Brother. Sifu would circle the rooftop, deep in thought, more often than not puffing on a cigarette, and sometimes he would speak to us; sometimes he would even show a technique or explain a concept, but mostly he just walked around.

It was only after some months, when I began to spend more time with him outside the class, that Sifu started to show and explain things to me in a deeper way. I realize now that I was fortunate I had no family ties in Hong Kong, and that working odd hours in the police force gave me greater access to Sifu. He was a powerful personality and a great influence, for bad as well as good, both inside and outside the martial-arts arena. I liked his numerous maxims, and made many of them my own.

He told me:

- 'Woman is the enemy of the hero' (so many women, so many enemies, so few heroes)
- 'If you don't rob somebody, somebody will rob you' (he robbed me of that holy trinity – time, energy and money).
- 'The mouth communicates, the mind interprets' (this was the last meaningful thing he taught me).

In recent years many of my Tai Chi brothers and sisters, while they admit the effectiveness of my approach, disagree with it. I am accused of changing things. Sifu told me, before I left Hong Kong, to do weapons in the way I do. He told me to practise Neigong more than form, as it would have a radical effect on all aspects of my Tai Chi. He told me to sink and root (Tai Chi parlance for lowering the centre of gravity to enhance balance) in everything I did, including pushing hands. He did not have just one way of doing things, but many ways, and I learned these ways as we travelled together in Hong Kong, Singapore, China, Malaysia, Australia and Britain.

Sifu told me not to be lazy like him – although I think his diabetes played a part in this; and to teach things personally as far as possible, so that people in the West could receive a true transmission. In all the 30 years I knew him, I never saw him do a complete form from beginning to end. He did practise some rolling on tatami mats and other conditioning, before he went abroad with me to teach, and sometimes he would push hands and wrestle with students in the class.

When he started out as a Sifu he was 19 years old and a renegade from the famous Tai Chi families; then he became successful through his ability to fight and produce fighters. This inspired me, when I returned to Europe, to follow his example. I strongly believed that there was a gap in the market to teach Tai Chi as a complete martial art, rather than as just a health exercise. I was right. I think of the things Sifu said and did in the old days and they help me to carry on.

The most inspirational martial-arts teacher, and probably the greatest martial-arts genius I ever met, was Yoshinao Nanbu. People don't talk much about him these days. I met Nanbu in January 1973, when he came to Glasgow to show our Shotokan club his Sankukai method. He did not hit or brutalize us, like the other Japanese whom we had encountered; he strolled around in his sunglasses, smiling at us. He captivated my interest with his whirling and spinning and, most of all, with his emphasis on evasion. He was by then a renegade and a legend. His master, Tani (of Shito-ryu and Shukokai fame), said years ago that he did not know any Nanbu.

My Tai Chi brother, Ian Cameron, saw Nanbu years ago, singing as he demonstrated Sai Kata while senior Japanese masters looked on in disapproval. Nanbu was the first and, as far as I know, the only Japanese master to compete in Europe. He always won because he said he would commit seppuku (ritual suicide) if he lost.

I visited Nanbu in Paris in 1974, just after he awarded me my black belt. I stayed in the dojo (martial arts training hall) of the famous Henri Plee, which is where I was to teach Tai Chi 20 years later. Plee told me that martial arts were like women: some of us could find the right one straight away, while others needed to try a few before they found the right one, and still others drifted from one to another like latter-day Casanovas. In the martial arts, at least, I have not become a Casanova.

Meeting these men of respect, men of the sword and of the pen made me want to become one. Maybe I now inspire others, too.

Masters

The term 'master' derives from the Latin root *magister*, meaning teacher or ruler; and, by extension, it means a person of consummate skill in some area of activity, as opposed to a mere journeyman. It can also mean someone who inspires devotion or reverence on the part of his or her followers. However, a person can be all or any of these things and yet fail to be a good teacher. There is only one measure of a good teacher: does he or she produce good students?

Many Tai Chi books refer to a golden age, when ancient masters were paragons of all the known virtues — invincible sages imbued with mystical powers. Yet these same masters lived and died like other men. Indeed, some famous members of the Yang family died of illness in middle age. Although ghosted books on Tai Chi Chuan have been produced by members of the major Tai Chi families, little has been added by the said family members to the said books to enrich the philosophy or literature of China.

Just as philosophers and ideologues throughout the ages have attempted to justify their ideas, however perverse or wicked, by recourse to the actions and words of thinkers of the past, so many modern masters analyse every thought and deed in the light of their often twisted and erroneous interpretations of the Tai Chi Classics. They would cloak everyone in the straitjacket of their rigid orthodoxies.

The ancient Chinese philosopher Mencius wrote that the evil of men is that they like to be the teachers of others, rather than trying to reform themselves first. According to Mencius, Confucius denied that he was a sage. And yet today many third-rate Tai Chi teachers call themselves 'master' or 'grandmaster'; some even dare to use the literary style 'zi' or 'tzu' after their names, in a vain attempt to equate themselves with the great philosophers of China, such as Laozi and Zhuangzi.

Tai Chi Chuan is often referred to as a Taoist martial art, and in many a book much innocent fun is made of Confucianism and the importance that it placed on rites and correct conduct. It is ironic that many such authors exhibit a far greater degree of rigidity and humbug than Confucius and his followers ever did. A cursory perusal of the *Analects of Confucius* shows that Confucian thinkers emphasized a natural ease in applying the rules of propriety. However, they also emphasized that in exhibiting this natural ease, the rules of propriety should still be followed — just as they should when interpreting and applying the guiding principles of the Tai Chi Classics.

The mad English king, George III, in one of his more lucid moments, observed that much of Shakespeare is sad stuff, only one mustn't say so. In the strife-torn world of internal martial arts there is a much higher proportion of 'sad stuff' than is to be found in the works of the Bard of Avon.

We have some masters without fighting experience speaking authoritatively on how to deal with opponents, and debating technical niceties. Others claim to be able to uproot opponents without touching them and, when their subtle skills fail to work, the fault lies with their insufficiently sensitive protagonists. Other masters put forward other people's ideas as their own, denigrate teachers of genuine ability and then lay claim to the same skills, without possessing any of them. Still others deny the existence and value of anything they don't know, while touting empty 'secret' techniques and training methods.

Having alluded to some of the more negative aspects of Tai Chi masters, I would now like to suggest some positive ones. A master in the true sense:

- Practises
- Leads by example
- Explains
- Constantly attempts to develop his or her art
- Constantly attempts to challenge students' perceptions in order to improve their understanding
- Teaches honestly and sincerely
- Is sufficiently harsh and sufficiently gentle with students.

By 'practising' I mean that the teacher should spend some time training with the class and also privately. In particular he should do the more physically and technically demanding training with his students, to give them confidence. When teaching, it is not enough just to issue commands; a martial-arts gym is not a drill square. And although we must practise drills, the students should be told the purpose of different exercises. When the teacher does not know this, he should say so and attempt to find out, rather than misleading his students. Anybody who purports to teach in exactly the same way as his own teacher cannot be considered a master, although he may be a competent instructor. Tai Chi is an art, and therefore to be a master you must be able to make it your own art, rather than merely copying another.

Experience is the greatest of all teachers, and to be a master you must be able to use your experiences to develop your art. By the same token you should provide your students with ways of developing their art. Competitions, books, videos and seminars can all aid in this process.

I believe that if a master does not wish to teach something to a particular student at a particular time, he should simply not teach it, rather then prevaricate or pretend to teach it. An insincere teacher will produce insincere students. Great masters do not necessarily make good men; good men do not necessarily make great masters. The fact that a master has many flaws in his personality does not make him any less of a master. The fact that an instructor is highly moral in character does not necessarily make him a more effective instructor.

Discipline and etiquette in Tai Chi classes are thorny questions. If too harsh and rigid, then the students will live in fear of the teacher. Of course some martial-arts students occasionally need to be criticized by the teacher – particularly when they are training in a way that is dangerous to themselves and / or others. Some students need strongly worded criticism from time to time; others require gentle encouragement. Students should not be treated the same unless they are the same.

In the Far East it is customary to address the teacher as 'Sifu' and to address fellow students as 'Elder / Younger Brother / Sister', depending on whether they learned before or after you. In my own classes I don't follow this procedure, and students call me Dan or (rarely) Mr Docherty. Some teachers require bowing both before and after each class, and when students take a partner for pushing hands or self-defence. My teacher never adopted this practice, and only required a student to bow to him and more senior members of the school when undergoing initiation as a disciple.

I much prefer this approach to that encountered in other schools, where they seem to spend as much time bowing to one another as they do training.

Four masters

Western people often have unrealistic expectations of Chinese Tai Chi masters, some of whom are very skilful at playing the role allotted to them. Yet, like us, they are only human and so, like us, they are imperfect.

What follows are warts-and-all pen portraits of four masters, including my own teacher, Cheng Tin-hung. In each case the karma they generated continues today. Two of them were major Tai Chi figures, one became a popular teacher and one lived in obscurity.

SINS OF THE FATHER

My esteemed friend, Dr Luce Condamine, once gave me a copy of the October 2004 issue five of the French martial-arts magazine *Dragon*, in which she was featured, teaching Tai Chi to children. There was also an interview with 79-year-old Yang Zhenduo, a fourth-generation master of Yang-family Tai Chi Chuan and the son of Yang Chengfu, the man largely responsible for Tai Chi's present-day popularity as a gentle system of exercise (largely because he travelled all over China to spread the art, and many of his students went on to become professional instructors themselves). Usually these old boys give fairly anodyne answers to sycophantic questions, or so I thought. However, the final question and answer were killers:

Dragon: 'Your father, Yang Chengfu, died at the age of 53. Under what circumstances?'

Yang Zhenduo: 'It followed an accident due to medication. My father found himself in South China, in Canton. He was a big strong man. He weighed 138 kilos (more than 300 lb)! Because of the heat, he was perspiring profusely. This perspiration gave him a kind of eczema at the level of his genitalia. In Hong Kong this causes fungus on the feet; it is a well-known malady. His nephew proposed that he use the normal medication for the feet, so he was given the product to put on his genitalia. The

Yang Chengfu

result was catastrophic. The product, which was in fact toxic, caused a swelling of his genitalia. He was urgently taken to Shanghai (a considerable distance), but medicine was not as developed as it is today and no one was able to save him.'

There is an element of the Oedipus complex about all this – whereby sons want to 'kill' their fathers and do unspeakable things with their mothers – but the story shows that naive stupidity has existed in the Yang family for at least two generations: on the part of the nephew for procuring and recommending the foot ointment; on the part of Yang Chengfu for believing that foot ointment was appropriate for rubbing onto the genitalia; and on the part of his son, Yang Zhenduo, for relating his father's ignominious end in a magazine interview. I hope my own son has something better to report, when the time comes.

'FRAGRANT HARBOUR' MASTER

I never met him. Cheng Wing-kwong, uncle and Tai Chi master to my own teacher, was dead long before I came to 'Fragrant Harbour'. I knew many who were his students (and thus my Uncles) in Malaysia, Singapore and Hong Kong. Everyone spoke well of him – a sure sign that he was no genius.

Before looking at the anecdotal and hearsay evidence, let us examine the writings. His one book, *Tai Chi Chuan Hui Pian* (*Tai Chi Chuan Compilation*), first came out in 1949, and the final version has five forewords, all written by respectable pals. Some of Cheng's students, such as Liu Kwong-sum and the enthusiastic but untalented Luk Siu-sun, also wrote books on Tai Chi.

Cheng was born in Niao Shi (Bird Rock) in Zhongshan County, Guangdong Province, in the Qing dynasty during the reign of Emperor De Zong (ruled 1875–1908). Though he was a good student, at the age of 13 he dropped his satchel in the harbour and was forced to leave the groves of Academe for the Fragrant Harbour world of commerce. He had the pen name Cheng Chek-wan.

His recurrent ill health was attributed to a lack of external physical action leading to internal problems. He therefore joined the Jing Wu (a Chinese health, fitness and martial-arts association, set up in Shanghai around 1910, with branches in Chinese communities around the world), took up the practice of Tai Chi and within a few months had recovered.

Hearing of the flight of renowned Tai Chi master Wu Jian-chuan to Fragrant Harbour from Shanghai in 1937, Cheng went to pay his respects and become his disciple at the earliest opportunity. In his five years with Wu, Cheng learned hand, sabre and sword forms, Tuishou (pushing-hand) skills and drills, a few applications and 20 of the 24 Neigong exercises. It was not a complete transmission, and yet he became Wu's leading Fragrant Harbour disciple.

After Wu's death in 1942 Cheng visited various teachers to sharpen his skills – some vicariously, as was the case with Qi Minxuan, whom he had brought from North China to teach his sons (who complained to their mother about Qi's brutality and were quickly excused) and his troublesome teenage nephew, Cheng Tin-hung. It was claimed that Cheng spent a bit of time doing Baguazhang with Sun Lutang (1860–1933), but this must been before he met Wu. Being a plausible fellow, Cheng was later to assure his students that Tai Chi included the Baguazhang technique 'Guangong Stroking his Beard'. It certainly did after he had finished with it.

Somewhere along the way – perhaps because he had a wife and two young concubines to satisfy – Cheng developed an interest in internal alchemy. His main master in such esoteric practices was (unsurprisingly) one of those nameless, itinerant Taoists who keep turning up in tales like this one. He learned the 'Muscle Change Classic' (Yijinjing) and 'Immortal Family Eight Pieces of Brocade' (Xianjia Baduanjin) from the said nameless, itinerant Taoist. The latter set of exercises is very far from the wholesome version taught by the official Chinese-health Qigong people. Cheng's book gives detailed instructions on the exercises in both of these Qigong sets, although there are no accompanying illustrations. His troublesome teenage nephew, unencumbered by wife or concubine and full of youthful vigour (years later he told me that when he went to Japan in the early Sixties he experienced clouds and rain with as many Nipponese women as he could get his hands on, in revenge for the Japanese occupation of China), was not a keen adept of internal alchemy and only taught it to three people. I was number three.

In 1953 Cheng set up the Wing-kwong Health Academy to pass on his knowledge and to benefit from the publicity generated by his book. With mainland China now given over to the establishment of Mao's peculiar brand of revolutionary Communism, this was one of the few Tai Chi books obtainable in Fragrant Harbour at the time. By this time Cheng's business activities were taking him round South-East Asia. Gradually he built up a network of contacts, some of whom became his Tai Chi students, especially in Malaysia and Singapore.

He was quite able to look after himself, and once bitch-slapped an obstreperous boatman into Fragrant Harbour using the Neigong technique 'Reclining Tiger Stretches its Waist', but he wasn't a fighter and had to ask his troublesome teenage nephew to come over and sort out a challenge from Wing Chun practitioner William Cheung and a couple of punk cronies. Troublesome nephew mowed down William with 'Sweep Lotus Leg' and William left with the punk cronies, having learned nothing, in pursuit of his own dark karma.

The pictures of Cheng doing hand form in his book show a certain easy, sedate quality and he is said to have been highly competent in Tuishou. His Neigong development was also considerable, and I have seen a photo of him taking a body-shot from the great boxer Joe Louis when he visited Fragrant Harbour. And the Brown Bomber could hit.

His troublesome nephew, Cheng Tin-hung, had learned Southern Boxing at a young age in Three Hamlets (San Xiang) from his grandfather, who said he would never make money by teaching it, but told Cheng to go to Fragrant Harbour and learn Tai Chi from his uncle, then teach rich and important people and become a success in the world. This he did. On his way he met Wu Jian-chuan, during his final years.

Cheng Wing-kwong and his nephew were initially quite close, but travelled different roads from 1947 onwards, when Qi Minxuan became Dutch uncle and Sifu to the nephew. Cheng's wife took the split badly and when the nephew and his students found fame and success at an international full-contact tournament in Taiwan, she sent a wreath.

I experienced every kindness from Cheng Wing-kwong's students during my visits to Singapore and Malaysia. Sifu Chow, from Singapore, gave us the finest ginseng from his pharmacy before we went to do combat on the Leitai (fighting platform), while Sifu Long Wei-tak from Kuala Lumpur bought us beer and curry and dispensed avuncular wisdom after the fights. Uncle Long had been an interpreter for the Japanese during the war; it wasn't something he was proud of.

As with most Chinese martial-arts tales there is a traitor – a hypocrite uncle by the name of Loong Fong, from Ipoh in Malaysia. When I played the role of second to bashed-up Tai Chi brother Tong Chi-kin in his quarter-final match in 1980 at the South-East Asian Chinese Martial Arts Championships, against the undefeated, Ipoh local, full-contact champion, a Chikechuan and Thai Boxing stylist, hypocrite uncle Loong Fong was there in support – in support of the undefeated, Ipoh local, full-contact champion. Guess he thought he was onto a winner when Tong got knocked down three times in the first round. But Tong was the bravest fighter I ever met and just kept coming. He broke the punched-out, undefeated, Ipoh local, full-contact champion. Hypocrite uncle Loong Fong then came over to get his photo taken with us. He was not made welcome. He later suffered the ignominy of dropping dead on a teaching trip to Sheffield. Poor Sheffield!

Quite a few senior UK teachers, such as David Barrow, Shelagh Grandpierre and Gary Wragg, trained in Cheng Wing-kwong's tradition at one time or another, and I hope if they read this, it might bring back a few memories. But I guess I was the only one to go tiger-hunting with shotguns and dogs in the Malaysian jungle with his uncles. It was back in 1981. I bagged a pheasant; it was tasty.

The late Richard Hughes, part barfly, part foreign correspondent, was one of many white demons who used the facile English translation of 'Fragrant Harbour' for Hong Kong. The correct translation is 'Incense Harbour'. Incense, both fragrant and carcinogenic when burned, is and was a major product and export from Hong Kong. With so much misinformation around, it's a wonder anyone knows anything.

It is more than 30 years since I ate ginseng before going to the Leitai in Kuala Lumpur. Cheng Wing-kwong, his troublesome teenage nephew and my uncles are all dead. What remains are me and some disaffected brothers. We'll do the best we can. Maybe some chronicler – maybe some brash nephew – will spin tales about us.

PREFACE TO AN INTENSIVE EXAMINATION INTO TAI CHI CHUAN

by Cheng Tin-hung, 1961, translated from the Chinese by Dan Docherty

'When the master taught me, he constantly emphasized the practical application of the art.'

My grandfather's personal name was Lin, and he was proficient in Southern Boxing, which he taught for a living. Our deceased father, (Cheng) Min-cheung, would teach us this boxing when we had finished our chores. When we grew older, our uncle (Cheng) Wing-kwong took an interest in me.

He put all his effort into practising the art of Tai Chi Chuan and Tai Chi Neigong and his character was well suited to this endeavour. Training day and night, he gradually absorbed the art, hoping to make himself outstanding amongst persons in the same field, so that he would not feel himself to be pitiable, even if it took him many years to achieve his goal. Though gradually to some extent successful, he had still not achieved perfection.

In midsummer 1946 he luckily met Master Zhi Meng (this is a Buddhist name meaning 'Sagacious Elder'). The master's secular name was Qi, and his given name was Min-xuan. He was from Wen County, Hebei Dao in Henan Province. He was well versed in the art of Tai Chi Chuan and the mysteries of Neigong. I felt very grateful that my master, when he visited Hong Kong, took a special interest in me and taught me all that he knew. When the master taught me, he constantly emphasized the practical application of the art. He himself would act as my opponent and order me to make use of Tai Chi Chuan techniques to dissolve his attacks, and furthermore to hit back at him. At that time I was in the prime of life, being young and vigorous. I found his methods deeply interesting. Morning and night I stayed with him under a relentless discipline, eager to obtain his secrets.

In the first month of winter 1948 he travelled north. When he was on the point of going, he told me that the original purpose of Tai Chi was to pay attention to following (that is, moving in concert with the actions of the opponent), so the external appearance does not emphasize daring and ferocity. Furthermore, recent generations of well-known Tai Chi families do not want to transmit the teaching of the practical application of the method and, as a result of this, successful men are few. This makes people despise Tai Chi Chuan.

He went on to say to me that if I wanted to gain a reputation in this art, not only must I be sound in mind and body, but also able to defend myself properly; because of this, and to allow the art to be transmitted to more people and develop, he said he did not dare keep anything secret from me.

Though I was ashamed of not being diligent and skilful enough, and of not yet attaining perfection, I had to follow my teacher's instructions to spread Tai Chi Chuan, to benefit the physical and mental health of students and particularly to help them understand the application of the techniques. I dare not be arrogant; if learned men come to teach me, I regard myself as very fortunate indeed.

A MAVERICK CHINAMAN

He was left-handed, heavy-set and of mercurial temperament. Cheng Tin-hung was born in the village of San Xiang in Guangdong Province in 1930 (or maybe 1928, if his claim in later years to have been born a dragon and not a horse was true). His grandfather, Cheng Lin, and his father, Cheng Min-cheung, taught Nan Chuan (Southern Boxing) to Cheng Tin-hung and other village youths. His grandfather, who also ran the local opium divan (a term we used in the Royal Hong Kong police), told him that he could never make a living from teaching Nan Chuan and advised the young Cheng Tin-hung to go to Hong Kong and learn Tai Chi Chuan from his uncle, Cheng Wing-kwong.

Following his grandfather's advice, he learned Tai Chi from his uncle initially and then from Qi Minxuan, who was invited to Hong Kong by Cheng Wing-kwong in the summer of 1946. Qi wasn't a professional Tai Chi teacher, but a landlord from Wen County, Hebei Dao in Henan Province. Cheng's uncle taught him the basics. Qi gave him the detail and taught him how to fight using Tai Chi. For two and a half years Cheng was Qi's personal student and followed Qi all over the hills and islands of Hong Kong, learning his Tai Chi in the great outdoors, using sticks and branches as weapons. In 1948 Qi returned to China and the revolution. They never met again.

In 1950 Cheng Tin-hung became a full-time Tai Chi instructor in Hong Kong at a time when many famous teachers were active there. The competition included Yang Sau-chung, Wu Kung-yi, Tung Ying-jie and Cheng Wing-kwong, his own uncle.

Cheng was known in his younger days as the 'Tai Chi Bodyguard', because he would stand up for Tai Chi practitioners everywhere with fist or weapon. He became famous throughout the South-East Asian Chinese martial-arts community in 1956 by defeating the three-times middleweight full-contact champion of Taiwan. He subsequently trained full-contact fighters who became Hong Kong and South-East Asian champions. Martial-arts journalists described what he taught as 'Practical Tai Chi Chuan', contrasting it with what other teachers were doing.

Cheng started Tai Chi teacher-training classes at the behest of the Hong Kong

Government's Sport & Recreation Department, to provide Tai Chi instructors for morning classes in the housing estates. He trained teachers to train other teachers. He wrote many books on Tai Chi, and taught millionaires and paupers alike. In his later years he retired to his village, a victim of blindness and congenital diabetes. He died in 2005.

Cheng Tin-hung

Tai Chi epiphanies

'"Epiphany" comes from the Greek word meaning a coming to light, an appearance, a revelatory manifestation of a god or divine being.'

I wouldn't have hit a youth in the kidneys on the London Underground platform if he hadn't, in his madness, been about to fall on my baby son. I had little choice and no time to think – I had to be in the moment, and hurt him with a static Tai Chi Neigong technique that I had never before used in that way. It was an epiphany.

The word 'epiphany' comes from the Greek word meaning a coming to light, an appearance, a revelatory manifestation of a god or divine being; it has therefore come to mean a sudden flash of insight into the essential nature of something or someone, or an intuitive grasp of reality. I have had a life full of epiphanies.

In the *Iliad* it is the gods who make the heroes blind to reason. The greatest hero in that book is Odysseus. He was not a god or even of divine descent; he was an ordinary man, but he always had a plan. He always tried to operate out of reason, not emotion. After so many years of blindness, I try to do the same.

Once I asked my Sifu to demonstrate applications to my students with sword against spear. He said, 'Impossible'; and so I did it myself. He had never thought of it because his old master had taught him only on the basis of sword against sword, or broadsword against spear. Of course, if he'd really been attacked, he would have had no problem in doing it. The late Robert Trias wrote a book called *My Hand is My Sword*; and my sword is also my hand.

My Russian friend, Albert Efimov, once took me to meet Konstantin V. Asmolov from the Russian Academy of Sciences. Konstantin is a geek, a typical Internet nerd: tall, thin, hunched and four-eyed. Nobody in Western Europe has heard of Konstantin, yet he is one of the most knowledgeable swordsmen you could ever meet. I had two hours in his company, talking and exchanging ideas and looking at ancient Chinese and Korean texts. I went home and the first time I picked up a sword, everything was new – I finally understood, and was like stout Cortez, silent on that peak in Darien with all his men, as he gazed for the first time on that lonesome ocean. Epiphany!

It is fairly obvious, when extending the arms or feet, that you are hitting your opponent; it is less obvious what is happening when you retract or coil them. Most people go through their whole Tai Chi career practising their forms without thinking about any of this. Practising like that is fine for producing a tranquil mind, but it will be difficult for them to advance their understanding of what they are actually doing.

It seems to me that the forms are arsenals of movement, and that these movements can be individually applied or combined together in an endless variety of combat possibilities. That is the value of forms; those old Chinese guys knew a few things, but we can't bring them back to learn what they knew. What we can do is practise with mindfulness.

Biodynamic Tai Chi

A few years back while visiting the Loire Valley in France I tasted different Vouvrays in the cellar of M. Huet, who produced them all using the '*Methode bio-dynamique*'. This method was developed by the Austro-Hungarian social philosopher and spiritualist Rudolph Steiner (1861–1925), who was the founder of anthroposophy, a spiritual and (to a degree) occult doctrine, which tried to understand the world by looking at the nature of man, rather than that of God.

Biodynamics is concerned with the dynamic relationship between organisms and their environment. For example, Steiner considered that in agriculture the use of pesticides and chemical fertilizers poisons the earth over a period of time; they are absorbed by plants such as vines through their roots, then are passed into the fruits of said plants (in this case grapes), which are then ingested by humans and animals. A recent survey of fruits and vegetables on sale in British supermarkets found chemical residue from pesticides and fertilizers in more than 25 per cent of the produce.

The essence of the Book of Changes is more than three thousand years old. The concepts of Yin and Yang are represented respectively by a broken line _ _ and an unbroken line ___. The broken line represents Earth and the vagina of the female, while the unbroken line represents Heaven and the penis of the male; the Earth is fertilized by rain falling from Heaven, which in turn causes plants to shoot their flowers up and their roots down. On a simplistic level, living organisms such as ourselves are composed of Yin and Yang, so we take our fuel in the form of breath and water from Heaven and our food from Earth and, after processing them in our bodies, we return the waste products to Heaven and Earth again. To maximize the absorption of these fuels, and therefore the amount of energy in the body, physical practices such as Qigong and Tai Chi Chuan became important, as did the place and time of practice.

Caves and mountaintops, because of their intimate connection with Heaven and Earth, became particularly popular places for practice. Indeed, the Tai Chi Chuan Classics invite us to be 'still as a lofty mountain and move like a great river'.

Our relationship with the natural world is pithily expressed in the various components of the Chinese characters representing Qi (vital force / energy), Jing (vital essence) and Shen (spiritual essence). Qi contains the rice plant (fundamental food) and so it is rooted to Earth and stretches to Heaven, with vapour given off when it is cooked; Jing contains the rice plant, as well as giving birth and the colour of plants; Shen shows the sun, moon and stars suspended from Heaven, and also depicts Humanity expanding outwards towards them. Various methods of breathing, combined with hygienic exercise, were developed to harness these Three Treasures and produce the ideal Taoist state of Heaven, Earth and Humanity in unity.

This combination of breathing and hygienic exercise was later combined with martial techniques, to produce the internal martial-arts forms and Qigong methods that exist today, including Tai Chi Chuan. When practising Tai Chi there is considerable emphasis on the body being rooted through the feet to the Earth and thus being well balanced, while simultaneously allowing the spirit to ascend by maintaining a straight (though not necessarily erect) line from the crown of the head through the spinal column to the tailbone, so that the central nervous system is correctly aligned and in order to develop abdominal breathing. In turn, this means that the interaction of the Three Treasures is enhanced.

The Tai Chi Chuan Discourse states, 'The root is in the feet' and talks about severing the root of the opponent. This rooting for balance is of crucial importance in pushing hands. For example, in fixed-step pushing hands the body is like a plant or tree (or any flower of your choice), rooted through the feet to the Earth, while the rest of the body sways and bends in accord with the elements (according to the way your partner / opponent responds). You can apply the same method of swaying with the head and upper body when using body evasion in self-defence. Equally, in both pushing hands and self-defence, you try to sever the root of your opponent in order to unbalance him or her and take advantage of the openings this provides. And in the sword form the technique of 'Turn Body Plant Sword' precisely involves sinking and rooting.

Many Tai Chi techniques express the deep relationship that practitioners of former times had with the natural (but not necessarily animal) world. From Neigong we have 'Embracing the One' (a reference to the unity of Heaven, Earth and Humanity) and 'Planting a Fence'. From the hand form there are 'Seven Stars' (Ursa Major or the Dipper), 'Cloud Hands' (a pun on the similar-sounding Chinese character for turning) and 'Sweep Lotus Leg'. For the sword the list includes 'Dispel the Clouds to See the Sun', 'Magic Hand Picking a Star', 'Shooting Star Chasing the Moon', and so on. The sabre has 'Cloud Sabre and Hiding the Sabre', 'Climb Mountain Look into Distance', Searching the Sea', and so on. Tai Chi spear contains 'Facing the Wind Blowing the Willow', 'The Waves Going Up and Down', 'White Rainbow Soaring over the Sun' and 'Plum Blossom Opens Five Petals'. In pushing hands we have 'Reeling Silk' (as if from a cocoon) and Cai Lang ('Uprooting Wave)'. Finally there are less well-known techniques such as 'Flying Flower Palm' and 'Five Element Arms' (Metal, Wood, Water, Fire and Earth).

It is true that Chinese martial arts and Qigong are to some extent based on animal movements, so we have 'Praying Mantis', 'Dog Boxing', 'Monkey Boxing', 'Dragon Sign', 'Snake Style' and so on, just as the spirit of the Tai Chi sabre is based on the tiger, while the spirit of the spear and sword is based on the dragon. Many Tai Chi movements are, however, based on dealing with animals rather than copying their movements, so we have 'Spin Around and Rein in the Horse', 'Catching a Giant Tortoise from the Bottom of the Sea', 'Embrace Tiger, Return [the tiger] to Mountain', and many more.

In recent years I have been running summer camps all over Europe. Weather permitting, this is a method of getting back in touch with the natural world. Even when training indoors I often switch off the lights. Our eyes and other senses were not designed to be stimulated constantly by light and other electrically produced sensations; computers, DVDs and mobile phones are pollutants twice over – in their production and in their action. So if you are going to practise Tai Chi, try to do so the biodynamic way.

Modern practitioners did not invent the art of Tai Chi, but we continue it. We have a duty to transmit it truly, so that future generations can express its beauty and efficacy as best they can, following the precepts of the Classics.

Conclusion

So how do you know whether you or someone else is doing good Tai Chi and having read the *Tai Chi Bible* where do you go from here?

The Chinese call their country 'Zhong Guo', the Central Kingdom.

We know from the Tai Chi Classics that the strength comes from the spine. Our bodies and minds always seek to be in a state of Zhong Ding / Central Equilibrium. We know we should be Zhong Zheng / Centrally Correct so that we can function optimally on a physical and spiritual level.

There is a Confucian classic called 'Zhong Yong' where Zhong is centrality and Yong means constancy. Put together, these characters are usually translated as 'The Doctrine of the Mean'. The idea is to do what is appropriate under any given set of circumstances. Zhong Yong is the answer to more than 90% of all possible questions about Tai Chi – and perhaps about life too. This type of discernment is refined by practise and experience.

How fast should I practise? How big should my movements be? In pushing hands how close should I be to my partner? In all cases Zhong Yong is the answer.

The Chinese term for Shen / Spirit is a composite character; one part represents the sky with the sun, moon and stars, while the other represents two hands extended. Rooted to the Earth below yet connected to Heaven above. This is Zhong Yong. This is the aim of Tai Chi. I wish you smooth winds on your journey.

Appendix:

Traditional Tai Chi Chuan Syllabus

The system from which this syllabus comes is sometimes referred to as 'Wudang Tai Chi Chuan' or 'Practical Tai Chi Chuan'; it is the full syllabus of my Sifu, Cheng Tin-hung. It can be considered part of the Wu style from the Yang lineage. Most Tai Chi teachers are not teaching a full syllabus, because they themselves have only received an incomplete transmission from their own masters. Most people don't have the capacity or time to learn a full syllabus anyway. I do teach a full syllabus, but most students lack the commitment to learn it all. It is set out below for the discerning reader.

The Tai Chi Chuan Classics

The Classics comprise five major texts, as follows:

- The Canon of Tai Chi Chuan
- The Fighter's Song
- Interpretation of the Practice of the Thirteen Tactics
- Song of the Thirteen Tactics
- The Tai Chi Chuan Discourse

The full texts are available in my book *Tai Chi Chuan: Decoding the Classics for the Modern Martial Artist*.

Neigong

Neigong (internal training) comprises 12 Yin and 12 Yang exercises:

- Golden tortoise
- Embracing the one
- Lifting a golden plate
- Jade rabbit facing the moon
- Red-capped crane stretching its feet
- Civet cat catching rats
- Flick the whip left and right
- White ape pushes out its paws
- Swallow piercing the clouds
- Leading a goat smoothly
- Giant python turns its body
- Elephant shaking its head
- Tiger paw

- Golden dragon coiled round a pillar
- White horse pounds its hooves
- Plant the fence left and right
- Wu Gang chopping laurels
- Rhinoceros faces the moon
- Reclining tiger stretches its waist
- Monarch of the mountain coming out from a cave
- Boatman rowing the boat
- Hungry eagle looking for food
- Macaque leaping through the trees
- Old man burning cinnabar

Pushing hands

Major fixed-step pushing hands (Tuishou) drills include:

- Four Directions (the forces Peng, Lu, Ji, An)
- Reeling Silk/Chan Si
- Bow Down, Look Up/Fu Yang
- Forearm Neutralizing/Zhou Lu

Major moving-step drills include:

- Four Corners (the forces Cai, Lie, Zhou, Kao – also called Eight Gates Five Steps, or Dalu/Big Neutralizing)
- Uprooting Wave/Cai Lang
- Seven Star Step
- Nine Palace Step

Tai Chi Long form

The movements are taught as Square Form, Round Form, Mirror Form and Reverse Form (Short Forms are also taught nowadays). The 48 Techniques in Chapter 4 encapsulate the essence of this Long Form. The names of hidden techniques are given in italics.

SECTION 1

1 The ready style (Wu Chi to Tai Chi)
2 The Tai Chi beginning style
   (Vanguard arms, Extend the arms)
3 The seven stars style
4 Grasping the bird's tail
5 The single whip
6 Flying oblique
7 Raise hands and step up
   (Single then Double seize legs)
8 White crane flaps its wings
   (Break arm style)
9 Brush knee twist step
10 The seven stars style left
11 Brush knee twist step (x 3)
12 The seven stars style left
13 Stroke the lute
14 Step up, deflect, parry and punch
   (Use the forearm to force the door)
15 As if shutting a door

16 Embrace tiger, return to mountain

17 Cross hands

18 Oblique brush knee twist step

19 Turn body, brush knee twist step

20 The seven stars style

21 Grasping the bird's tail

22 Oblique single whip

SECTION 2

23 Fist under elbow

24 Step back and repulse monkey (x 3)

25 Flying oblique

26 Raise hands and step up

27 White crane flaps its wings

28 Brush knee twist step

29 The seven stars style left

30 Needle at sea bottom

31 Fan through the back

32 Turn body and swing fist

33 Step back, deflect, parry and punch
   (Use the forearm to force the door)

34 Step up, grasping the bird's tail
   (Reverse seven stars)

35 The single whip

36 Cloud hands (turning hands)

37 The single whip

SECTION 3

38 Pat the horse high left

39 Left drape body *(Separate hands)*
   (Tiger embraces head)

40 Right separate feet

41 Pat the horse high right

42 Right drape body
   (Separate hands)
   (Tiger embraces head)

43 Left separate feet

44 Turn around and kick with the heel

45 Brush knee twist step (x 2)

46 Step forward and plant punch

47 Turn body and swing fist

48 Step up and pat the horse high left

49 Left drape body
   (Separate hands)
   (Tiger embraces head)

50 Right separate feet

51 Step back seven stars style

52 Step back to strike the tiger

53 Drape the body and kick

54 Box the ears

55 Right drape body
   (Separate hands)
   (Tiger embraces head)

56 Left separate feet

57 Turn body and kick with the heel

58 Swing fist

59 Step up, deflect, parry and punch
(Use the forearm to force the door)
60 As if shutting a door
61 Embrace tiger and return to mountain
62 Cross hands
63 Oblique brush knee twist step
64 Turn body, brush knee twist step
65 The seven stars style
66 Grasping the bird's tail
67 Oblique single whip

SECTION 4

68 The seven stars style
69 Parting the wild horse's mane
70 The seven stars style
71 Parting the wild horse's mane (x 3)
72 The seven stars style
73 Parting the wild horse's mane
74 Fair lady works shuttle (x 2)
75 The seven stars style
76 Parting the wild horse's mane
77 Fair lady works shuttle (x 2)
78 The seven stars style
79 Grasping the bird's tail
80 The single whip
81 Cloud hands (turning hands)
82 The single whip

SECTION 5

83 Snake creeps down
84 Golden cockerel stands on one leg
(right) *(White snake spits out tongue)*
85 Step back and repulse monkey
*(Golden cockerel stands on one leg
left) (x 3)*
86 Step aside, flying oblique
87 Raise hands and step up *(Double
seizing legs)*
88 White crane flaps its wings
89 Brush knee twist step
90 The seven stars style left
91 Needle at sea bottom
92 Fan through the back
93 Turn body and swing fist
94 Step up, deflect, parry and punch
(Use the forearm to force the door)
95 Step up grasping the bird's tail
(Reverse seven stars)
96 The single whip
97 Cloud hands (turning hands)
98 The single whip

SECTION 6

99 Pat the horse high left

100 Slap the face

101 Cross and single hand sweep lotus leg

102 Brush knee twist step

103 Step up to punch the groin

104 Step up, grasping the bird's tail (Reverse seven stars)

105 The single whip

106 Snake creeps down

107 Step up, seven stars

108 Step back to ride the tiger

109 Turn body and slap the face

110 Turn body and double hand sweep lotus leg

111 Draw the bow to shoot the tiger

112 Pat the horse high left

113 Slap the face

114 Turn body and swing fist

115 Step up to pat the horse high

116 Step up, grasping the bird's tail

117 The single whip

118 Tai Chi in unity

119 Completion style

Scattering hands

Scattering Hands (Sanshou) in Chinese martial arts refers to self-defence applications, which include the following subdivisions:

Die Pu – to make the opponent fall and then hit him (or hit him so that he falls)

Shuai Jiao – grappling techniques, including throwing, sweeping and tripping

Qin Na – seizing and holding, including locking and grip strike-techniques

Dim Mak (Dian Xue) – attacking vital points with locks, strikes and so on.

48 SANSHOU APPLICATIONS

1 Seven stars style

2 Grasping the bird's tail

3 Single whip

4 Flying oblique high and low

5 Raise hands and step up

6 White crane flaps its wings

7 Brush knee twist step

8 Stroke the lute

9 Deflect, parry and punch

10 As if shutting a door

11 Embrace tiger, return to mountain

12 Cross hands

13 Fist under elbow
14 Step back and repulse monkey
15 Needle at sea bottom
16 Fan through the back
17 Swing fist
18 Cloud hands
19 Pat the horse high
20 Drape body left and right
21 Separate feet left and right
22 Turn body and kick with heel
23 Step forward up plant the punch
24 Turn body and swing fist
25 Step back seven stars
26 Beat the tiger
27 Drape body and kick (also known as
   Two raisings of the foot)
28 Box the ears
29 Parting the wild horse's mane
30 Fair lady works shuttle
31 Snake creeps down (low style)
32 Golden cockerel stands on one leg
33 Slap the face
34 Single hand sweep lotus leg
35 Punch the groin
36 Step back to ride the tiger
37 Double hand sweep lotus leg
38 Draw the bow to shoot the tiger
39 Double seizing legs
40 Break arm style

41 Gyrating arms
42 Tiger embraces head
43 White snake spits out tongue
44 Vanguard arms
45 Flying flower palm
46 Five-element arm
47 Running thunder hand
48 Single seizing leg

Note that the following pairs of
techniques are very similar: 17 (Swing
fist) and 24 (Turn body and swing fist);
1 (Seven stars) and 25 (Step back seven
stars); 39 (Double seizing legs) and 48
(Single seizing leg). However, in yet
another unexplained (and presumably
inexplicable) anomaly there are six
distinct techniques in the form that are
not named as applications in the above
list and these are:

Beginning style

Completion style

Separate hands

Extend hands

Use the forearm to break the door

Step up seven stars

Weapon forms

(all weapon forms are trained on both sides)

TAI CHI SABRE FORM

The sabre form is called Xuan Xuan Dao. Xuan means mysterious and 'Xuan Xuan' was a nickname for Zhang Sanfeng, the legendary founder of Tai Chi; Dao means a sabre/single-edged weapon.

1 Ready style

2 Tai Chi beginning style

3 Grasping the bird's tail

4 Brush knee twist step

5 Separating the sabre

6 Dodge and display the sabre

7 Picking a star on the left

8 Advance to tease the genitals

9 Withdraw to divert with the sabre

10 Pierce the heart

11 Hang the golden bell on the left

12 Push open the window to watch the moon

13 Swivel and chop

14 Swivel and tease the genitals

15 Hanging the golden bell on the left

16 Climb the mountain to look into the distance

17 Sparrow hawk turning around

18 Peng spreading its wings

19 Swallow entering its nest

20 Advance and divert with the sabre

21 Stab the face

22 Swivel hiding the sabre

23 Point to the trousers with the sabre

24 Chop the tiger

25 Swallow entering its nest

26 Advance and divert with the sabre

27 Pierce the heart

28 Swivel hiding the sabre

29 Above three opening style

30 Taking off the boots when drunk

31 Lying fish style

32 Cloud sabre and hiding the sabre

33 Stab the face

34 Turn around and chop

35 Searching the sea

36 Retrieving the moon from the sea

37 Hanging the golden bell on the left

38 Opening the window to watch the moon

39 Seven stars style

40 Hungry tiger jumps over the stream

41 Stab the face

42 Lying tiger style

43 Hiding the sabre style

44 Pierce the heart

45 Coiled dragon

46 Coiled dragon stepping quickly

47 Lying fish style

48 Cloud sabre and hiding the sabre

49 Pierce the heart

50 Lying tiger style

51 Lying fish style

52 Cloud sabre and hiding the sabre

53 Stab the face

54 Lying tiger style

55 Lying fish style

56 Cloud sabre and hiding the sabre

57 Pierce the heart

58 Swivel and chop

59 Searching the sea

60 Sweeping a thousand soldiers

61 Picking a star on the left

62 Chop the tiger

63 Returning horse carrying a bell

64 Embracing the moon

65 Rowing the boat with the current

66 Flying oblique style

67 Advance and chop with the sabre

68 Swivel and chop

69 Searching the sea

70 Sweeping a thousand soldiers

71 Shooting star chasing the moon

72 Chop the tiger

73 Cloud dragon playing in the water

74 Swivel and chop

75 Advance and chop

76 Hiding the sabre style

77 Pierce the heart

78 Picking a star on the left

79 Return the sabre style

80 Brush knee twist step

81 Tai Chi in unity

82 Finishing style

TAI CHI SWORD FORM

The sword form is called Qian Kun Jian –
'Heaven and Earth Sword'.

1 Tai Chi beginning style

2 Grasping the bird's tail

3 Golden needle pointing south

4 Passing the sword style

5 Spreading the sword style

6 Hanging the sword style

7 Intercepting the sword style

8 Rhinoceros watching the moon

9 Step up to protect the knee

10 Swivel and dot

11 Turn back and stab

12 Hanging the golden bell upside down

13 Point to the trousers with the sword

14 Male and female phoenix
spreading wings

15 Shooting star chasing the moon

16 Li Gwong shooting an arrow at a tiger

17 The wheel on the left and right

18 Fisherman casting his net

19 Spin around and rein in the horse

20 Step up and move towards the door

21 Step back coiled dragon

22 Face to face sword

23 Yellow dragon turning right

24 Pui Kung cleaving a snake

25 Shooting star chasing the moon

26 Li Gwong shooting an arrow at a tiger

27 Embracing the moon

28 Pierce the heart

29 Step back and tease the genitals

30 Tiger lying in front of the door

31 Steersman rowing the boat

32 Rowing the boat with the current

33 An immortal pointing the way

34 Dot red between the eyebrows

35 Cross the knees and chop

36 Step up to tease the genitals

37 Embracing the moon

38 Pierce the heart

39 Hang the bamboo basket on the left and right

40 Fairy damsel throwing a needle

41 Turn back raising the writing brush

42 Face the door sword

43 Tiger lying in front of the door

44 Catching a giant tortoise from the bottom of the sea

45 God of literature raising the wine vessel

46 Swing the arm back with the sword

47 Turn the body and plant the sword

48 Flick the whip on the left and right

49 White gibbon offering fruit

50 Tiger lying in front of the door

51 Fallen petals waiting for the broom

52 Tiger lying in front of the door

53 Turn back to put on armour

54 Swivel with the sword

55 Encircling the moon

56 Single whip style

57 Hanging the golden bell upside down

58 Sweep a thousand soldiers on the left and right

59 Advance and point to the trousers

60 Scaly dragon hiding and about to fly

61 Green dragonfly touching water

62 Swivel and tease the genitals

63 Cloud signal flag three times

64 Advance with reverse cut

65 Dispel the clouds to see the sun

66 Magic hand picking a star

67 Left and right horsetail broom is blown by the wind

68 Fierce tiger jumping over the stream

69 Remove the leg and intercept

70 Fish lying down on the left and right

71 Spin and sweep across

72 Yellow dragon turning left

73 Spreading aside the grass looking for a snake

74 The wheel on the left and right

75 White snake putting out its tongue

76 Peng spreading its wings

77 Rein in the horse to watch the tide

78 Encircling the moon style

79 Single whip style

80 Sparrow hawk piercing the forest

81 Peng spreading its wings

82 Peasant digging with a hoe

83 Face the door sword

84 Spin and sweep across

85 Shooting star chasing the moon

86 Spin and sweep across

87 Great grandfather fishing

88 Support the beam and replace the column

89 Golden needle pointing south

90 Tai Chi in unity

91 Sword completion style

TAI CHI SPEAR FORM

The spear form is called 'Thirteen Techniques Spear', referring to techniques 3–15 in the following list:

1 Ready style

2 Tai Chi beginning style

3 Facing the wind blowing the willow

4 The waves going up and down

5 Obstructing the river to intercept the dipper

6 Green dragon stretching its claws

7 Giant python turning its head

8 Golden dragon swinging its tail

9 Giving the horse its head while chasing enemies

10 The black-eared kite flies and the fish leaps

11 Golden cockerel nodding its head

12 A white rainbow soaring over the sun

13 Lying tiger and diving dragon

14 Plum blossom opens five petals

15 Celestial horse walks the skies

16 The completion style

Note that weapon forms are also learned and performed as Mirror Form. There are also two-man weapon forms: sword versus sword, sabre versus spear, and so on.

Six Secret Words

These words represent practical fighting concepts and are taught to advanced students:

- Lend/borrow
- Vibrate
- Torque
- Slice
- Clap
- Lever

Auxiliary training

In addition to the technical syllabus, there are numerous other training and conditioning methods, both with and without partners. Like many other instructors, I also teach a Qigong system, but that is not Tai Chi, so it lies beyond the scope of this book.

Bibliography

A Book of Five Rings by Miyamoto Musashi, translated by Victor Harris. Overlook Press, 1974.

A Brief History of Qi by Zhang Yu Huan and Ken Rose. Paradigm Publications, 2001.

A History of Chinese Philosophy by Fung Yu-lan. Princeton Paperback Printing, 1983, Volumes I & II.

Asian Fighting Arts by Donn F. Draeger and Robert W. Smith. Berkeley Publishing Corporation, 1969.

Chang San-feng Ch'uan-Chi (The Complete Works of Chang San-feng) Wong Shiu Hon, Australian National University Press, 1982.

Chen Style Taijiquan. Hai Feng Publishing Co, 1984.

Chinese Boxing: Masters and Methods by Robert W. Smith. North Atlantic Books (USA), 1974.

Chinese Characters by Dr. L. Wieger. SJ. Lucky Book Co. Reprint of 1927 edition.

Complete Tai Chi Chuan by Dan Docherty. Crowood Press, 1997.

I Ching, Translated by James Legge, Bantam Press, 1969.

Imagination Becomes Reality by T.T. Liang. Bubbling-Well Press Co, 1984.

Lost T'ai-Chi Classics from the Late Ch'ing Dynasty by Douglas Wile. State University of New York Press, 1996.

Myths and Legends of China by E.T.C. Werner. Published by Graham Brash in Singapore, 1984

Nei Wai Gong Tu Shuo Ming Ji Yao by Xiao Tian Shi, Published by Zi You Chu Ban She.

Original Tao by Harold D. Roth. Columbia University Press, 1999.

Outlines of Chinese Symbolism & Art Motifs by C.A.S. Williams. 3rd Revised Edition, Dover Publications.

Pao Chui by Gu Liu Xin. Published by Hai Feng Chu Ban She, 1986.

Pilgrims and Sacred Sites in China, edited by Naquin. The University of California Press, 1992.

Scholar Boxer by Marnix Wells. North Atlantic Books, 2005.

Science & Civilisation in China vol. V by Joseph Needham. Cambridge University Press, 1983.

Self and Society in Ming Thought by Anna Seidel. Columbia University Press, 1970.

Sexual Life in Ancient China by R.H. Van Gulik. Brill, Leiden, 1974.

Sources of Chinese Tradition vol. I & II compiled by Wm. Theodore de Bary & others. Columbia University Press, 1960.

T'ai Chi's Ancestors by Douglas Wile. Sweet Ch'I Press, 1999.

T'ai Chi Ch'uan by T.T. Liang. Random House, Inc, New York, 1977.

Tai Chi Chuan Da Wen by Chen Wei Ming, Published by Tai Bei, Hua Lian Chu Ban She, 1981.

Tai Chi Chuan – Decoding the Classics for the Modern Martial Artist by Dan Docherty. Crowood Press, 2009.

Tai Chi Chuan Hui Bian by Zheng Rong Guang. Published by Wu Shu Chu Ban She.

Tai Chi Chuan Jing Jian by Cheng Tin Hung Bian Zhu. Published by Cheng Tin Hung Tai Chi Jian Shen Xue Yuan Chu Ban.

Tai Chi Chuan Shi Yi by Dong Ying Jie. Published by Hong Kong Hua Lian Chu Ban She.

Tai Chi Chuan Shu by Gu Liu Xin. Published by Zhong Guo Tu Shu Kan Xing She, 1985, 1986.

Tai Chi Chuan Shu Yao by Cheng Tin Hung Bian Zhu. Published by Hong Kong Tai Chi Association.

Tai Chi Chuan Xue by Long Zi Xiang. Published by Hong Kong Jing Hua Chu Ban She.

Tai Chi Chuan Xue by Sun Lu Tang. Published by Hong Kong Wu Shu Chu Ban She.

Tai Chi Chuan Zhi Li Lun Yu Shi Yong by Zhong Zi Ruo. Published by Tai Bei Shi "Zheng Zhong Shu Ju", 1975.

Tai Chi Chuan Zhi Yan Jiu by Ma You Qing. Published by Shang Wu Yin Shu Guan Hong Kong Fen Guan, 1984.

Tai Chi Sabre, Sword, Spear by Cheng Tin Hung Bian Zhu. Published by Tai Chi Shan Zhuang.

Tang Song Yin Yang Wu Xing Lun Ji by Punin, Luo Gui Cheng. Published by Hong Kong Gong Cheng She, 1982.

Tao Te Ching, translated by D.C. Lau. The Chinese University Press, Hong Kong, 1963, 1982.

The Book of Balance and Harmony by Thomas Cleary. Rider, 1989.

The Book of the Sword by Richard F. Burton. Dover Publications, New York, 1987.

The Chart of Tai Chi Chuan by Tseng Chiu Yien. Union Press Limited.

The Chinese Knight-Errant by Liu James. J.Y. Routledge and Kegan Paul Ltd., 1967.

The History of Tai Chi Chuan by Danny Vercammen. Dao Association, 1991.

The Life of Marpa the Translator. Shambhala, 1999.

The Origin and Dissemination of Chinese Characters by L.Wu. Published by Caves Books, Ltd. 1990.

The Shorter Science & Civilization in China: vol. I & II by Ronan and Needham. Cambridge University Press, 1978, 1981.

The Taijiquan Classics, An Annotated Translation by Barbara Davis. North Atlantic Books, 2004.

Bibliography

Wu Jia Tai Chi Chuan by Wu Gong Zao. Published by Hong Kong Jian Quan She Chu Ban Xiao Zu, 1980, 1981.

Wu Shi Tai Chi Chuan by He Shao Ru. Published by Ren Min Ti Yu Chu Ban She, 1963.

Wu Shi Tai Chi Chuan Tui Shou by Ma Yue Liang, Xu Wen. Published by Shanghai Shu Ju Youxian Gong Si Chu Ban, 1986.

Wu Style Taijiquan by Wang Peisheng and Zeng Weiqi. Published in Hong Kong, 1983.

Wudang Song Xi Pai Nei Jia Quan by Wang Wei Shen. Published by Hong Kong Hai Feng Chu Ban She You Xian Gong Si, 1989.

Yang Style Taijiquan. Hai Feng Publishing Co, 1988.

Glossary

I've rendered most of the Chinese expressions in the Glossary in modern Mandarin *Pinyin* romanization. In a few cases where the Cantonese or another Mandarin romanization system is more common in reference to a term I have given that. Unfortunately a number of Chinese characters sound the same, but have quite different meanings creating possible pratfalls for the non-Chinese reader. I've done my best in this Glossary and in the text to give the major Chinese terminology and explanation in the hope that this is clearer than vague English translations for what are essentially technical terms.

An – downward directed push/press

Baduanjin – Eight Pieces of Brocade. Chinese soft exercise for health sometimes including techniques to stimulate the reproductive system.

Ba Gua / Pa Kua – Eight Trigrams, consisting the four cardinal points and four corners.

Ba Gua Zhang – Eight Trigram Palm; internal martial art based on Eight Trigrams.

Bai Shi – ceremony of ritual initiation.

Bao Yi – to embrace the one (i.e. the *Tao*).

Bu – Footwork and stances.

Cai – a plucking or uprooting force.

Chan – School of Budhism with heavy Chinese influences; better known in the West by its Japanese name of *Zen*.

Chang Chuan – Long Boxing. An alternative name for Tai Chi Chuan as well as the name given to a hard style boxing form.

Chi/Qi – Vital energy, including the air and breath. (N.B. not the same Chi as in Tai Chi!).

Chi Kung/Qi Gong – a method of training designed to increase the vital energy, for martial, health or meditative purposes which can be hard or soft in nature.

Chien – Trigram / hexagram representing Heaven and Supreme Yang.

Ching/Jing – Classic or Book.

Chuan/Quan – Fist. By extension a system of fighting or boxing.

Da Lu – Great sideways diversion. Popular name for famous pushing hands exercise more properly known as Four Corners or Eight Gates Five Steps.

Dan Tian/Tan Tien – cinnabar field, area just below the navel where Chinese alchemists considered internal energy was developed.

Dao – The sabre.

Dim Mak/Dian Xue – Vital point attacks.

Gong/Kung – Work / effort involving a degree of skill. In Chinese martial arts this usually refers to various types of conditioning training.

Hsing I/Xing Yi Chuan – Form and Intent Boxing; one of the three major internal styles.

I Ching/Yi Jing – Book / Classic of Change. A book of divination dating from before 1000 BC in one form or another.

Ji – Straight line force.

Jian – Sword.

Jin/Jing – Force. We listen for our opponent's Jin and redirect it with our own before discharging Jin at our opponent.

Jing – vital (often seminal) essence. (N.B. not the same Jing that means force).

Kao – To lean. Applying force using the shoulder or back.

Kung Fu / Gongfu – Skill / effort / workmanship. Often used by Cantonese speakers and Westerners to refer to Chinese boxing.

Lao Shi – Old (i.e. venerable) teacher. Term of respect for teacher or master.

Li – Strength.

Lie – Spiralling force.

Lu – Diverting an oncoming force to the side and into emptiness.

Men Ren – Door Person. One who has become a disciple of a master.

Mian Chuan – Cotton Boxing. Early name for Tai Chi Chuan.

Nei Jia Chuan – Internal Family Boxing. Including such arts as *Tai Chi Chuan, Ba Gua Zhang* and *Xing Yi Chuan*.

Nei Dan – Internal alchemy.

Neigong/Kung – Internal Strength. More specifically a reference to the 24 Yan and Yang Internal Strength exercises.

Pai – School of thought / boxing.

Pao Chui – Cannon Punch. Name given to Chen Family boxing and to their second form.

Peng – Upwardly directed force, e.g. to divert a push upwards.

Qiang – Spear.

San Shou – Fighting techniques. Can also refer to choreographed two person forms or to Chinese full contact fighting.

Shaolin – referring to the Buddhist temples of that name in Henan and Fujian provinces and by extension to external martial arts identified with these temples.

Shen – Spiritual energy.

Shi San Shi – Thirteen Postures / Tactics. an old name for Tai Chi Chuan.

Shi – Style. e.g. Hao Shi – (Tai Chi Chuan) in the style of Hao.

Sifu/Shifu – Teaching father. By extension any teacher or highly skilled person.

Song – Relaxed.

Tai Chi/Taiji – The Supreme Pole / Ultimate composed of Yin and Yang.

Tai Chi Chuan/Taijiquan – A system of martial arts and exercise based on Yin and Yang.

Tao – The Way or Ways to enlightenment or self development followed by the Taoists.

Tao Te Ching – Way and Virtue / Power Classic. Prime Taoist text credited to Lao Tzu (the Old Boy).

Tui Shou – Pushing hands. Various partnered drills and exercises designed to improve skills such as close quarter control of an opponent, evasion coordination etc. Can also refer to free or competition pushing hands, where the object is to unbalance the opponent.

Tu Di – Student or apprentice.

Wu Ch /Ji – No Ultimate. State before Tai Chi.

Wudang – Referring to the mountain of that name.

Wai Dan – External alchemy. The use of medicines and by extension a reference to internal martial arts.

Wai Jia – External family referring to hard style martial arts.

Wu Shu – Martial arts. Nowadays this Mandarin term has come to be used mainly in reference to the highly acrobatic and artistic modern martial arts routines.

Yang – Active, male, positive principle representing strong, hard, external, bright, day, Heaven etc.

Yi – The intent.

Yin – Passive, female, negative principle representing gentle, soft, internal, dark, night, Earth etc.

Zhen Chuan – True Transmission from a master to a disciple.

Zhen Ren – True Person. Someone who by Taoistic methods has become a sage.

Zhong Ding – Centrally Fixed corresponding to the element Earth.

Zhong Yong – Doctrine of the Mean, text of the Confucians. Philosophical concept of acting only to the degree necessary, neither more nor less.

Zhong Zheng – Centred and straight (though not necessarily upright).

Zhou – The use of the forearm or elbow in defence or offence.

Zu Shi – Founding teacher. Zhang San-feng.

Index

Acknowledgements

I'd like to thank the few who were chosen to help me produce the *Tai Chi Bible*. Firstly Professor Ladan Niayesh, the world's smartest Persian, from the Sorbonne, Paris, who helped me with the structure as well as appearing in some of the photos. My feisty chum, Dr. Alex Ryan, from the University of Gloucester made useful suggestions on presentation. Birgit Muller, Germany's top red-headed geographer, did a great job on the diagrams and line drawings. Viktoriia Talashchenko, Ukraine's leading Cossack, assisted with typing and admin.

European Tai Chi Championships double gold medallist, 'MagicMagyar' Gabriella Kosa, posed for all of the form and most of the application photos in a superb display of her versatility. Other models include long-time assistants Clifford Cox, Steve and Kathy Davies as well as Catherine Birkinhead, Rae Brunton, Neil Farnan, Jason Tsang, Damien Hoadley-Brown and Mark Paterson. I'm deeply grateful to all.

Finally many thanks to the good people at Octopus for their professionalism and understanding.

Any errors or omissions are entirely my own.